Mallo

CLEO

Timmy
Scout
Sugar!
Gerald
Napoleon
Sasha
Paddy
Cheeky
Murphy
Sherlock
Seeny
Rayston
Dinky Jones
Fluffy
Smokey
PINKY
MR ED
Snooky
Tabitha
MISTY
PEANUTS
JET
Sooty
Cleo
WELLINGTON
MAX
CELIA + SMOKEY
Novo

Cat-a-List

A Compendium of Interesting and Unusual Cat Names

compiled by

Dick Henrywood

with illustrations by

Colin Petty

The Bucklebury Press

First published in 1991 by
The Bucklebury Press

Text R.K. Henrywood and the Bucklebury Press 1991
Illustrations Colin Petty 1991

ISBN 1 871667 01 1

Printed in England by Wessex Press (Wantage) Ltd.
Artwork Scanned and Computer Typeset by Wessex Computing Ltd

Introduction

Pets have long played an important part in our domestic lives, and both cats and dogs would form major ethnic groups if they were to be included in census returns. The domestic cat, in particular, is the object of love and affection, and most cats are treated as if they are fellow humans. They seem to understand our rather one-sided conversations, even if our naïve attempts at training are studiously ignored. Indeed, cats are an enigma dependent yet independent, aloof yet companionable their main purpose in life seems to be leading us humans a merry dance, and we love them for it!

Our fascination with cats has led us to give them every possible type of name. Perhaps the easiest to understand are those based on colouring, Ginger and Blackie for example, or Tiger for a tabby, but these account for only a small proportion.

In the following pages you will find names derived from religion and mythology, from serious literature and popular fiction, from foreign languages, the arts, the sciences, the performing arts, and finally from pure ingenuity and word play.

Particularly popular are those names chosen by children from books and cartoons. Some of the more adult names recall famous (or infamous) people from ancient times to the present day, and there are also placenames from the four corners of the earth. Some cats are named after other animals, a lion cub, a racehorse, and even a killer whale. And some cats, of course, are themselves named after other cats; it is difficult to imagine a 'cat'-egory which is not represented.

Despite all the careful thought which goes into choosing their names, the cats themselves don't seem to care overmuch. They just continue to float serenely through our lives, leaving us bemused but much enriched. We hope this small tribute will help repay them in some way for all the pleasure they have brought to us. Long may they pros-'purr'!

A

Aba

Not the mis-spelt name of a Swedish pop group, but simply short for abandoned. The name belongs to a cat from Cheltenham who lives with several interesting companions, including Safran and Sandal.

Abby

A typical pet name, belonging to a male Abyssinian from Chingford whose full pedigree name is Adreesh Love-in-a-Mist.

Abigail

This tabby from Plymouth is usually known as Abbie. The full name was derived from the mineral galena, inspired by the owners' interest in geology. Galena, or bleischweif, is lead sulphide in the form of grey cubic crystals. It is distributed throughout the world and is the commonest ore of lead.

Adkribu Boniface

The very formal name of a lilac point Burmese from Addington, near Croydon. He is more usually known by his nicknames Teddy or Teddward the Terrible.

Adreesh Morning Sparkle

As with many pedigree cats, the formal name (this an Abyssinian from Chingford) is usually ignored. He is more affectionately known by his pet name of Junior, often shortened to just June.

Agata

A female blue point Siamese from Oxford whose owner is a prolific writer in the artificial language Esperanto. Agata is derived from *agato,* the Esperanto word for agate, chosen to reflect the cat's colouring.

Alabama

Named by a girl in honour of her current boyfriend's enthusiasm for American country and western music.

Albert

Not an uncommon name, but earned by a cat from Nottingham for quite an original reason. Although actually called Pudding, he grumbled and moaned constantly, just like the character Albert Tatlock in the long-running TV series *Coronation Street.*

Ali

A grey stray who came to live in the alley beside his new owner's house in Chigwell, quite literally an alley cat. Another patchwork beauty called Ali was found abandoned in a rubbish bin in Putney and named after an actress as she seemed convinced a contract was just around the corner if she preened herself long enough! Ali MacGraw (b.1938), the American actress, rose to fame in 1971 in the film *Love Story.*

Amadeus

This musically inclined cat seems most content in front of the fire listening to Mozart. Wolfgang Amedeus Mozart (1756-1791), born in Salzburg, was a child prodigy and went on to become the most famous composer of music in the Viennese or classical school. Oddly enough Mozart was not christened Amadeus, his real names were Johannes Chrysostomus Wolfgangus Theophilus.

Ambarita

A female tortoiseshell cat from Madrid whose full name is actually Ambarita Tarka Del Rey. Ambarita refers to the colour of her eyes and is derived from the Spanish word *ambarina,* meaning amber-like.

Amber

The name of this black cat from Plymouth was inspired by the owners' interest in geology. Amber is a fossilised resin formed from certain pines which flourished in Oligocene times.

Ambrose

At least one cat is named after the popular bandleader Ambrose. Bert Ambrose (1897-1973) began his musical career as a violinist but went on to lead one of the best British bands of the wartime years and formed a classy big band in the early 1950s to record for MGM. His theme was 'When Day is Done'.

ANDY CAPP

Amy

There must be many cats called Amy, amongst them one named by a mineral enthusiast after the precious stone amethyst. Another is a tabby christened as a kitten just because she seemed old-fashioned and a fuss-pot; no offence intended to any real life ladies with the same name!

Andy Capp

This grey and white cat from Horsham was named because of a prominent grey-pointed cap in his head markings. His amorous exploits have earned him the nickname Randy Andy. Andy Capp is the lazy and belligerent cloth-capped hero of the comic strip created by Reg Smythe which first appeared in the *Daily Mirror* in 1957 but is now widely syndicated.

Annapurrna

An irresistible urge to climb the curtains earned this kitten a fun name incorporating a pun on the word purr. Annapurna is in Nepal and rises to some 26,545 feet. Although not as high as Everest, about 190 miles to the east, it must still be one of the best known mountains in the Himalayas.

Anwyl

A cat from Madeley near Crewe whose name is derived from *anwylyd,* the Welsh for beloved.

Aphra

This fiercely independent female tabby from Oxford is named after a woman writer of great interest to modern feminists. Aphra Behn (1640-89) served as a spy in Antwerp during the Anglo-Dutch war of 1666-7, but was unrewarded and imprisoned briefly for debt in 1668. She then turned to writing for a living, at first mainly plays, but later also prose fiction and poetry.

Ardezo

Another of the Oxford cats owned by a writer in Esperanto. Ardezo is a male seal point Siamese and his name is the Esperanto word for slate, again chosen to reflect the cat's colouring.

Arizona A.J. Adventurepuss

A compound name for a black and white tom from Batley in Yorkshire. Arizona was selected from enthusiasm for America and its placenames; A.J. in honour of an American TV character much admired when the owner was younger; and Adventurepuss because the cat is an inveterate explorer.

Arthur

Particularly well-known as the cat in television adverts but a less distinguished namesake lives on Merseyside. This Arthur is the grandson of Sir Noshalot and has inherited his prodigious appetite, thus earning the nickname Jaws.

Attila

As a kitten Attila seemed to spend his entire existence terrorising his brothers and sisters. Attila the Hun (c.406-453) was a warlike king known as the 'scourge of God'. He controlled much of central Europe, overran the Balkans, invaded Gaul and Italy, and caused considerable devastation.

Axminster

A most original name for a kitten who, like the famous Axminster carpets, had a deep pile coat and was always 'underfoot'. The carpet factory at Axminster in Devon was founded by Thomas Whitty, a cloth weaver, in 1755. The factory itself only survived until 1835 but the name is still widely used for a particular type of machine-made carpet.

BANDIDO

Badger

The full name of this black and white tom from Edinburgh is Brock Badger, because of his colouring. Nowadays he is usually known just as Badger since he is constantly badgering his owners for food.

Bandido

A black and white tom from Ibiza, named by friends of the owner because of headmarkings which make him look as if he is wearing a bandit's mask.

Barnaby

One cat called Barnaby is named after the pathetic title character in Charles Dickens' book *Barnaby Rudge* (1841). Another tom with the same name is described by his owner as a 'cool cat'.

Basil and Sybil

A pair of cats named after the two leading characters, played by John Cleese and Prunella Scales, in the BAFTA award-winning TV comedy series *Fawlty Towers* (1975, 1979). The names are sometimes found individually, one cat called Basil is a grey half-Siamese from Aberdeen.

Baska and Gibi

Turkish names from a household in Bath, these two were named to reflect their colouring in comparison to one of their brothers. *Baska* means different from and *gibi* means like, or similar to.

Beaujolais

A name chosen for a smoke cameo from Chelmsford just because it had an onomatopaeic ring. It was eventually shortened to Beau, and then to Bo Diddley and finally to Diddles, because he was the smallest of the litter.

Beauregard

This cat seemed to have a military bearing and was given the name of an American soldier. Pierre Gustave Toutant de Beauregard (1818-93) was born in Louisiana and served in the American army through the Mexican War. He resigned to fight for the Confederates in the Civil War, became a General, and later held public office in New Orleans.

Bedsox

A name based on markings, closely related to Boot, Clogs and Socks.

Beeb

This is simply a nonsense name belonging to a tabby cat from Somerset adopted from the RSPCA. He was meant to be called Rhubarb, the imagined conversation between the new cat and the resident dogs, but the owner's young granddaughter couldn't manage the word so it became Beeb.

Bees Knees

A female tortie-white from Crawley who beats up all the neighbourhood toms and whose proper name is Bramble. The nickname Bees Knees came about because she always gave the impression that she was far superior to all other cats which, of course, she is!

Bella

This female chocolate Burmese from Hockley in Essex was actually named after a friend's golden-brown koi carp that was exceptionally friendly. The name is more usually a diminutive of Thumbelina.

Bellamy

Bellamy is a tabby and white tomcat from Mansfield in Nottinghamshire. He acquired his name after a rabbit which was always lagging behind in a sketch which appeared in the TV comedy series *The Goodies*.

Betty Beatrix Bouvier

A mock pedigree name for a moggy from Tisbury in Wiltshire. It was chosen partly in honour of the children's author Beatrix Potter (1866-1943), and partly after the American first lady Jackie Kennedy (b.1929), later Jackie Onassis, whose maiden name was Bouvier.

Biber and Tuzlu

Two more cats from the household in Bath, again with Turkish names. These two were named after their colouring, *biber* meaning pepper, and *tuzlu* derived from the Turkish for salt.

BEES NEES

Bilbo Baggins

This stray from Fowey in Cornwall was found curled up in a hole in the hedgerow. He was named after the most famous of the hobbits, furry creatures invented by J.R.R. Tolkien whose homes were holes in grassy banks. Bilbo Baggins is the main character in *The Hobbit* (1937) and also appears in *The Lord of the Rings* (1954-5).

Billy Brown

Billy Brown is a black and white tom from Laindon in Essex, originally one of a series of stray cats each of which was known as Billy. He acquired the surname from his new owner, a widow whose husband had also been called Billy.

Billy Bunny Corkhill

A cat from Tisbury in Wiltshire, named mainly after the electrician Billy Corkhill, played by John McArdle, in the popular TV series *Brookside*. The other part of his name arose from his bunny-hopping method of coming downstairs.

Binglet

Just a fun-sounding nickname for a lilac Burmese from Rochdale.

Biscuit

A fairly common colour-related name, adopted for a British blue from Newbury amongst others.

Bisley

Another of those names chosen just because it seemed to fit. The inspiration was a black and white poster which had recently made an impression on the owner.

Black and Dekker

A pair of black cats, the first named Dekker after the lead singer in the Jamaican pop group Desmond Dekker and the Aces. Their biggest success was the song 'Israelites' in 1969. When a second black cat arrived, the couplet of Black and Dekker proved irresistible.

Black Harry

One of three visiting tomcats from Cheltenham, referred to as Tom, Dick and Harry. The black one logically became Black Harry.

Bo Diddley

This name belongs to a smoke cameo from Chelmsford. He was originally called Beaujolais but that was altered to reflect his status as the smallest in the litter. Bo Diddley (b.1928), real name Ellas McDaniel, became one of the most influential rhythm 'n' blues artists of the 1950s, a source of inspiration to many later rock groups such as the Rolling Stones.

Bodica Britannia

A verbal and autocratic cat from Maulden in Bedfordshire, named after the famous domineering queen. Boadicea (or more correctly Boudicca) was the Queen of the Iceni tribe. She is best known for her revolt against the Romans, and is supposed to have taken poison after her defeat by the governor Suetonius Paulinus in AD 62.

Bog

Perhaps the most uncomplimentary cat name ever invented. It is the nick-name of a black and white tom from Lanarkshire who used to be extremely dirty and smelly.

Bomber

This was the first choice for a fluffy tabby from Northampton, thought originally to be a tom, and was selected because the cat seemed to zoom everywhere. When the owners discovered their mistake, she was renamed Bon-Bon.

Bonnet

A Welsh stray who is lucky to be alive. He earned his name after surviving some thirty miles crouched on the battery under the bonnet of a car.

Bonneville

Bonneville

One of at least four names inspired by motorcycles, this Cornish cat from Fowey named after the favourite bike of the owner's late husband. The first Triumph machine appeared in 1902 and the 650 cc Bonneville was introduced in 1959. The name is derived from the famous stretch of salt flats in Utah.

Bonnie and Clyde

A pair of pure white cats from Bury St Edmunds, named after the title characters in the well-known gangster film because they were an inseparable pair of hell-raisers and villains as kittens. *Bonnie and Clyde* starred Warren Beatty and Faye Dunaway and was first released in August 1967.

Bono Belly

This fat tomcat from Wiltshire was named in part after the vocalist in the pop group U2. Bono was born Paul Hewson in 1960, and the group was formed in Dublin in 1977. They were regarded as one of the best new rock bands of the eighties.

Boosey and Hawkes

A pair of cats named by a musician after a well-known London firm of musical instrument makers and publishers.

Boot

Another name based on markings, closely related to Clogs and Socks. Boot is tabby and white with a distinctive boot on one front leg. Her name was inspired by the scruffy old English sheepdog in Maurice Dodd's strip cartoon *The Perishers,* and she lives in Somerset with a companion called Maisie.

Boz

A female black cat from Gloucestershire, whose name was inspired by *Sketches by Boz*, a collection of stories which are some of the earliest literary works by Charles Dickens, first published in various periodicals but assembled in book form in 1836-7. Boz was used as a pen name by Dickens, particularly when writing *The Pickwick Papers*.

Bracken

Another name based purely on colour association, the cat's fur being reminiscent of the distinctive brown of dying bracken in the autumn.

Brahms and Liszt

A brother and sister from London, both brown tabbies. The names are Cockney rhyming slang and the owner liked both the association with drink and the composers. Johannes Brahms (1833-97) was German and Franz von Liszt (1811-66) was Hungarian; both were pianists and conductors as well as composers.

Bramble

Bramble is a relatively common name for black cats. One female kitten from Glasgow acquired the name since she looked and felt so much like the brambles (the Scots name for blackberries) that her owner had been picking.

Brewster

A name chosen at random for one cat amongst many in a household at Corsock in Scotland.

Brût

One of a pair of Ocicat x hybrids from Grimsby whose names were inspired by the aftershave Brût, a favourite of the owner's husband. The other is called Fabergé.

Bugsy

Bugsy is a long-haired cream Persian found abandoned and frightened under a stationary car in Bridgwater. He was rescued by the RSPCA and named after the state in which he was found, filthy and dirty with tangled fur infested with fleas.

Bumble

One of a pair of red tabby twins from Northampton, named after his looks large, dopey and usually horizontal!

BOMBER

Burma

A male red/orange Burmese from Failsworth in Manchester, given an obvious name to reflect his origin.

Buster

This belongs to a very large black tom from Brinsley in Nottinghamshire, originally named Sooty and chosen at the cat home because he looked so pathetic yet greeted his new owners with a very loud purr. He was renamed Buster when he developed into a big bruiser, although he has not one malicious bone in his body.

Butterfly Kiss

A blue tortie Burmese from Melksham with a cream "kiss' mark on top of her forehead, given a name to match.

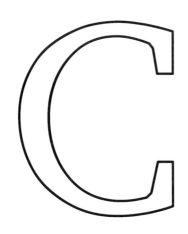

Caesar

CAESAR

There are a number of tomcats called Caesar. Gaius Julius Caesar (100-44 BC) was a Roman general and statesman who invaded Britain twice and later became dictator of the Roman empire. He was murdered on the ides of March by a group of nobles including Brutus and Cassius.

Cagney and Lacey

Two cats named after the title characters in the American TV detective series. *Cagney and Lacey* first appeared as a TV movie starring Loretta Swit and Tyne Daly in 1981. The theme was developed into a popular series although Loretta Swit was initially replaced by Meg Foster and then by Sharon Gless.

Caliban

A black stray who came to be fed and was originally far too fearful to venture very close, but eventually presented his benefactor with a mouse as a thank you. Caliban is a savage and deformed semi-human slave in Shakespeare's romantic drama *The Tempest,* which dates from 1611.

Calypso

Calypso is a tortoiseshell from Edinburgh named with a neat combination of her owner's dance and sailing interests. The calypso, the well-known West Indian song and dance rhythm, was also the name of the oceanographic research ship commanded by Jacques Cousteau (b.1910). He invented the aqualung in 1943 and won three Oscars for his underwater films.

CAPONE

Cantuar

The Anglican Archbishop's latin signature, adopted by one breeder as a prefix for a whole string of cats. Most have the relevant Latin names such as Carliol (Carlisle), Cestr (Chester), Dunelm (Durham), Ebor (York), Elien (Ely), Londin (London), Norvic (Norwich), Roffen (Rochester), Sodor Man (Isle of Man), and Winton (Winchester).

Capone

A particularly appropriate name for a cat from Bedfordshire who was an absolute villain. Alphonse Capone (1899-1947) was born in Brooklyn and became a gangster in Chicago, achieving worldwide notoriety during the prohibition era. He escaped prosecution until 1931 when he was convicted of tax evasion and sentenced to ten years in jail.

Casco

An appropriate American name for a Maine Coon kitten from Bath. Casco is a resort town in Casco Bay, about 25 miles north of Portland in Maine. The bay covers the area between Cape Elizabeth and Cape Small and contains over 200 islands, many of them summer resorts.

Casper

Casper is named after the friendly baby ghost which joined a team of cops in the American cartoon series *Casper and the Angels* (1980).

Catley Bodkin

An educated tabby from Oxford named after the Bodleian Library at the university. He was originally called Bodley Catkin, to mean the little cat of the Bodleian, but his name was soon spoonerised. He used to perform an amazing dance to beg for cheese spread on a spoon.

Cayenne

One of three kittens from Gloucestershire whose mother was called Chilli Pepper. The other two are named Paprika and Pepperoni.

Cellar

Cellar is a black and white tom discovered as a wild kitten with two others in a cellar in Portsmouth Dockyard. He now lives near Southampton and has grown into a beautiful and very tame cat.

Chancer

A grey tabby from Co. Antrim, found abandoned in a cardboard box. She was originally called Little Miss No Name but soon became Chancer because at times she 'pusshed' her luck too far.

Charana Prettyboy

This blue Burmese from Melksham was named by a British Airways pilot after two airways location indicators. Charana is a customs station in Western Bolivia, on the border with Chile. The Prettyboy is a dam and reservoir built in 1933, about twenty miles north of Baltimore in Maryland.

CATLEY BODKIN

Chephren

A name given to a lilac Burmese from Rochdale for sentimental reasons, following a memorable holiday in Egypt which included a trip to the pyramids. Chephren, also known as Khafre, was the third Pharaoh of the fourth Egyptian dynasty, reigning c.2850 BC. He was the builder of the second pyramid at Giza, and possibly also the Sphinx.

Chesney

The full name of this male cat from Tisbury in Wiltshire is actually Eric Argus Chesney Herbaceous Border. The Chesney part is after Chesney Allen (1894-1982), the popular light comedian who partnered Bud Flanagan from 1924 as Flanagan and Allen. They were also both members of the Crazy Gang (1937-59).

Chester

A large, dignified cat who is basically a coward, named after Chester Tate, the male lead with similar characteristics in the television series *Soap* (1977-82).

Chigley

This black and white everyday moggy from London was given a name that just seemed to suit her. She is also insultingly known as Shoddy Body.

Chilli Pepper

A female tortoiseshell and white cat from Gloucestershire. Obviously a red hot momma since she had three kittens called Cayenne, Paprika, and Pepperoni.

Chivers

A marmalade cat with a name inspired by its colour resulting from a visit to the grocer's shop to buy some Chivers orange marmalade.

Chivers and Greaves

A pair of moggies from the east end of London, named by a Tottenham Hotspur football supporter after Martin Chivers (b.1945) and Jimmy Greaves (b.1940), two famous strikers of the mid-1960s.

Christy

One of very many cats which have been rescued by the PDSA. She now lives in Northampton but was named after passing the Christmas lights outside the Derry & Toms store in Kensington High Street on the way home.

CALYPSO

Chuch

A tabby and white cat found in the streets of Moscow but now living in London. She was originally called Tucha, which sounds like the Russian for cloud, after the way she 'floated around' as a kitten. Later on she became hyperactive and her name changed to Chuchelo, the Russian for scarecrow, eventually shortened to just Chuch.

Chui-Chai

Chui-Chai is a female Siamese from Ashford in Middlesex, named after a Siamese dance. The owners chose the name to remind them how she led them a dance when she was born.

Circe

A name from Greek mythology for a female cat with a rather mysterious character. Circe was a mythical sorceress, powerful in magic, who attempted to use her charms to conquer Odysseus.

Claude

Claude is a male tabby and white from Mansfield, one of those polydactyl cats with extra claws.

Clawed de Pussy

A rather fine double play on words, chosen for another cat who seemed to be over-endowed with claws. Achille Claude Debussy (1862-1918) was a composer, regarded as a leader of the ultramodern school of music in France.

Cleopatra

The Egyptians worshipped their cats and this is not an uncommon name. Cleopatra was the Queen of Egypt for twenty years (51-30 BC), best known for her exploits as mistress to both Caesar and Anthony, and for her dramatic death, supposedly poisoning herself with an asp.

Clogs

Another of the names based on markings, closely related to Boot and Socks. Clogs comes from Bedfordshire and once again has distinctive white stockings. The name was also inspired by the owner's Dutch in-laws.

Clover

A female tabby from Glasgow, named after the colours of the clover flower. She turned out to be a very lively kitten and her name eventually trans'mog'rified to Popocatepetl.

Coco

Coco is the name of a chocolate point Siamese from Chippenham nicknamed Chocolate Boots, and also of a long-haired black cat from London. The latter spends her time protecting her virginity from local males but they have all been neutered and must think she is a bit whacko. Gabrielle Chanel (1883-1971), known as Coco, is one of the legendary figures of the twentieth century. She was a French couturier who revolutionised women's fashion in the 1920s and again in the 1950s.

Cole

A black cat named after the famous American composer and lyricist. Cole Porter (1891-1964) has been described as the greatest songwriter of this century, responsible for songs such as 'Anything Goes', 'Begin the Beguine', 'From This Moment On', 'I Get a Kick Out of You', 'I Love Paris', 'It's All Right With Me', 'Just One of Those Things', 'Too Darn Hot', and many others.

Condor

Another colour association, this time a brown cat whose name was derived from the well-known pipe tobacco.

Connie

A tortoiseshell cat from Chigwell in Essex who was brought back from a summer holiday in Cornwall. The new owners felt that Connie from Cornwall seemed a nice bit of alliteration.

Cooking Fat

Cooking Fat must be the most common spoonerism used as a cat's name. It seems to be particularly popular in the north of England.

Cosmo

A rather battered black stray tom living in Ibiza. His name Cosmo was taken from the phrase 'Cosmo's going up town', used by Sylvester Stallone playing Rocky in the film *Gasoline Alley*.

Cuddly-Dudley

This nickname for Dudley Moore, the comedian, actor and pianist, belongs also to a tabby and white tom from Mansfield. Dudley Moore (b.1935) was a member of the original Beyond the Fringe team and rose to fame in 1965 for his TV appearances with Peter Cook in *Not Only But Also*. He has since starred in many films, including *Ten* and *Arthur*.

Currant Bun

Currant Bun is a grey abandonee from London, actually named Sylvester but nicknamed due to prominent spots on his stomach. The name hardly worries him since he is deaf as a post, having fallen from a fourth floor window earlier in life. He usually ignores expensive cat food in favour of rummaging through dustbins for potato peelings!

Cushy

A cat owned by a lover of folk music and named after a famous Geordie character called Cushy Butterfield. In recent years the song about her has been adapted for use in a television advertisement for Newcastle Brown Ale.

Cyrus

An appropriate name for a long-haired grey Persian cat from Castle Douglas in Scotland. Cyrus the Great was King of Persia (550-529 BC) and founder of the Persian Empire.

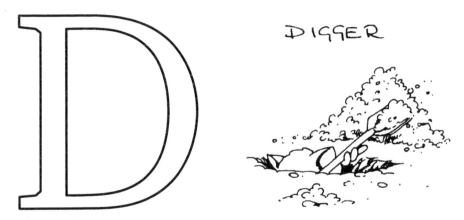

DIGGER

Daisetta Star

This blue tortie Burmese from Melksham is another of the cats named by a British Airways pilot after airways location indicators. Daisetta is a small town about 100 miles north east of Houston in Texas.

Daisy Bell

Daisy Bell is a black and white female from Fowey in Cornwall. She is named after a daisy because she has yellow eyes and lives out in the garden most of the time.

Danny

Danny is a blue Burmese from Hockley in Essex and was originally named after the popular Irish song 'Danny Boy', written by Fred E. Weatherly (1848-1929). He has since been nicknamed Big Daddy Dan as he is growing into a very big cat!

Decay

A long-haired cat from Aberdare, described by his owner as being as black as decay. Known as DK for short, he has two sons called Donner and Blitzen.

Del Rey

The full name of this tortoiseshell cat from Madrid is actually Ambarita Tarka Del Rey. The Del Rey part is after the street in which she lives.

Dempsey and Makepeace

A pair of cats named after the television detectives. The series *Dempsey and Makepeace* was introduced in 1985 and featured a London policewoman, played by South African born Glynis Barber, partnered by an American cop, played by Michael Brandon.

Demus

Demus lives in London and his name is short for Nicodemus, chosen because he is black and slim, like a little demon. Nicodemus was the ruler of the Jews who appears in St John's Gospel. The name was adopted much later for the Gospel of Nicodemus, an apocryphal book about Jesus, much used by writers of miracle and mystery plays.

Diamond Disc

A Bedfordshire kitten born on the day its owner had an operation for the removal of a disc.

Digger

This cat either thought he was a dog and loved bones or was convinced he was in a prison camp. He just couldn't stop digging all the time!

Dirty Dick

An (occasionally) white British cat from Aberdeen. The original Dirty Dick was Nathaniel Bentley (c.1735-1809), a well-to-do merchant who was crossed in love and then let his life degrade into miserly squalor. His hardware store in Leadenhall Street became famous for dirt and decay, and some of its contents were bought by a publican to decorate his tavern in Bishopsgate known as Dirty Dick's.

Don-Juan

One of several Esperanto-related forenames belonging to a Siamese cat usually known as Monte, this one in honour of the Canary Islander Juan Régulo Pérez, a professor of languages and an important Esperanto publisher.

Donner and Blitzen

A pair of cats from mid-Glamorgan who were named when their owner was taking a German conversation course. The names are German for thunder and lightning, and are perhaps best known as two of the companions of Rudolph the red-nose reindeer.

Donut

Donut is the long-haired son of an Olympia champion, and his name was derived from cream donut, reflecting his fur colour. He lives in Kent and insists on his own territory, which includes a den in the garden clearly marked 'Donut's Doze Area'.

Dusty Boy

The pet name of a short-haired black cat from Nottinghamshire actually named Buster. His thick black coat was noticeable for very easily showing dust. Another tabby and white tom from Lincoln is named Dusty for a similar reason.

Dynamite

Dynamite, black and explosive, was extremely energetic as a kitten; he used to tear all over the place as if his tail was on fire.

DEMPSEY

ERiC AND ERNiE

Echo

As a kitten this female brown tabby from Aberdeen was noticed to mimic every noise made by a companion cat called Quincy.

Elizabethan

One of the names of a cat from Wiltshire, delightfully christened Lettuce Elizabethan Lily Pod Trout! This part is derived from the fur around her neck, rather like an Elizabethan ruff.

Elwood

Elwood and his partner Jake are named after characters from the film *The Blues Brothers*. Made in 1980, it has recently become a popular cult movie.

Eric and Ernie

Two tabby and white cats from Mansfield named after the immensely popular entertainers Morecambe and Wise. Ernie Wise (b.1925) and Eric Morecambe (1926-84) are best remembered for their television shows, and were both awarded the OBE in 1976.

Eric Argus

A tomcat from Tisbury in Wiltshire whose full name is actually Eric Argus Chesney Herbaceous Border. The Argus part refers to the 100-eyed giant in Greek legend.

Ernfrid

Another Esperanto-related forename belonging to a Siamese cat usually known as Monte, this one in honour of Ernfrid Malmgren, a Swedish past-president of the Universal Esperanto Association.

Estopen

This must surely be a unique name, belonging to a cat from Ealing. Her owners lived in staff quarters at a hospital where there were many resident cats, and the kitten was collected at the same time as a prescription from the dispensary. Estopen is a proprietary trade name for penethamate hydriodide, a type of penicillin.

Eswyn

A tomcat from Teddington in Middlesex, named after the road in which he was found living wild. He now delights in the pseudo-pedigree nickname Eswyn Wesley Warburton Junior.

Etta

Etta is one of several slightly old fashioned girl's names favoured by cat lovers. It belongs, amongst others, to a tortoiseshell from Cheltenham who was named in memory of a previously owned tortoise called Henrietta. Perhaps the most appropriate derivation concerns a cat whose father was always believed to be the local tom called Henry.

JAKE AND ELWOOD

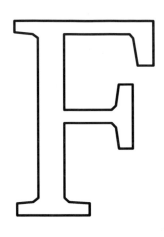

Fifi

Fabergé

One of a pair of Ocicat x hybrids from Grimsby. Their names were inspired by the popular aftershave Brût, made by Fabergé, a favourite of the owner's husband.

Faggot

A tabby cat from Swindon whose name was inspired by a delicious smell of cooking which wafted through from the kitchen when she was collected by her new owners. She has a companion called Haggis.

Fanny-by-Gaslight

This chocolate point Siamese lives on Jersey and was originally named Skye. She earned this nickname because she wantonly exposes her tummy every time she wants to be tickled.

Fat Cat

Fat Cat is a tabby living at Crawley whose real name is Chloe. This nickname developed in recent years along with her somewhat portly shape, although the owner notes that she can still waddle with considerable speed and grace.

Felis

This female cat belongs to a librarian from Winchester, Felis being simply the Latin name for the cat genus.

Felix

This must be one of the earliest names recorded in modern times for a domestic cat. Felix was one of the first cartoon cats, created by Otto Messmer in 1919 and drawn by Pat Sullivan in the 1920s. A black tomcat, with mannerisms based on Charlie Chaplin, he appeared in cartoon films and comic strips through to the 1950s and is still popular today.

Ferenc

One of several Esperanto-related forenames belonging to a Siamese cat usually known as Monte, this one in honour of Ferenc Szilágyi, a Hungarian writer and author of Esperanto textbooks.

Fergus

A ginger cat from London, named"for Gus', the kind Scotsman who found a nice home for him when the time came to leave the litter.

Fester

Fester is named after one of the characters in the American TV series *The Munsters*. The programmes were made in 1964 and 1965 and were followed by the film *Munster Go Home* in 1966.

Fiamma

A red point Siamese from Wales with another of the names taken from a foreign language, this time chosen by an owner who lived in Italy. The word means flame, and has a nice double connotation since it applies both to flame in the sense of fire, for the cats colouring, and also in the context of affection 'an old flame'.

Fifi

A self-explanatory name for a brazen hussy of a cat from Bedfordshire, totally without morals.

Filo

Filo is a truly yuppy blue point Siamese from Thetford, named after the proprietary personal organiser Filofax.

Flavius

A lilac point Siamese which was found abandoned on a street corner in New York and named after a friend's eccentric uncle who lived in Arkansas.

FOSBURY

Floss

Simply a pet name, in this case an abbreviation of Kandi-Floss, belonging to a female cream Burmese from Hockley in Essex.

Floydd

A tabby and white tom from Mansfield whose name was remembered from a phrase in an old Toffo advert 'Go get 'em Floydd!'

Fosbury

An athletic cat named after the famous high jumper. Richard Fosbury (b.1947) was 56th in the world rankings in 1967 but won the Olympic gold medal in 1968 using a revolutionary new technique. Executed backwards, it quickly became known as the Fosbury Flop and is now virtually universal.

Frank and Betty

A pair of cats from Walthamstow who were originally to be called Kettle and Saucepan, but that was vetoed by grownups. Their new names were taken from the main characters, played by Michael Crawford and Michele Dotrice, in the popular TV comedy series *Some Mothers Do 'Ave 'Em*.

Freckles

This self-explanatory name is purely a reflection of the cat's unusual markings.

Fred

The simplest of names, probably fairly widespread, chosen by one child who was very keen on the character Fred Flintstone from the animated TV cartoon series *The Flintstones*.

Freeman, Hardy and Willis

Three kittens taken in by the RSPCA. They quickly found a new owner who originally intended to take only two of them, but when the names Freeman, Hardy and Willis were suggested, after the High Street chain of shoe shops, all three were given their new home together.

Freida

Freida was a sickly little kitten when rescued but is now a healthy multicoloured and stubborn ball of fur who lives in London. She insists on eating her meals up on the kitchen counter, above the other feline hoi polloi!

Frisky

Maybe not the most distinctive of names, but a ginger and white cat from Kent earned it for an unusual reason. It was one of five ginger stray kittens born in the body shell of a kit car which was taking some time to assemble. The kittens were only discovered when they emerged to play 'King of the Castle' on a tree stump. Frisky was the manufacturer's name for the car.

Fungus

A name inspired by the lovable yet repulsive title character in Raymond Briggs' children's book *Fungus the Bogeyman* (1977).

Furry Face of this Parish

An extremely British nickname for a cameo Persian who is actually resident in Spain.

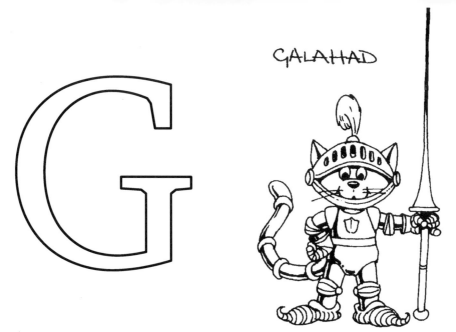

GALAHAD

Galahad

Galahad is a pure white cat from London, named after the knight as a symbol of purrfection! In Arthurian legend Galahad was the son of Lancelot and his chastity was rewarded by a sight of the Holy Grail (the chalice used by Christ at the Last Supper), and a seat at King Arthur's famous Round Table.

Gandalf

A big, grey, furry cat named after J.R.R. Tolkien's famous wizard. Gandalf the Grey first appeared in *The Hobbit* (1937) and subsequently became one of the main characters leading the fight against the dark forces in *The Lord of the Rings* (1954-5).

Garfield

Cartoon cats are inevitably popular, and the name Garfield has been adopted for a tabby and white tomcat from Mansfield, probably along with many others. Garfield is the fat ginger cat in the comic strip of the same name by the American cartoonist Jim Davis, dating from 1978. Modern marketing has made him one of the most successful comic characters of the past decade, featured in some 1,200 newspapers.

Gata

Gata is a tomcat owned by a librarian from Winchester. His name is particularly simple, just the Greek word for cat.

Ghost

A pure white ball of fur with a name inspired by the phrase "ghostly white'.

Gizmo

Simply a nickname for a black and white cat from Batley in Yorkshire.

Golde

A long haired grey and white cat from Sidcup, one of eight named by an enthusiastic amateur dramatist after characters in *Fiddler on the Roof*. The American premiere was in 1964 and it ran for 3,242 performances in New York and for 2,030 performances, with Topol in the leading role, in London. It was the Drama Critics' Best Musical in 1965 and includes the popular song 'Sunrise, Sunset'.

Goldie

This predominantly gold tortoiseshell cat from Surrey was given a name inspired by an American actress. Goldie Hawn (b.1945) achieved fame in the comedy series *Rowan and Martin's Laugh-In* (1968-70). She won an Oscar for best supporting actress in *Cactus Flower* (1969) and was nominated for best actress for the title role in *Private Benjamin* (1980).

Goofy

The runt of a litter of five, a female tabby from Horsham named because of her sweet but dazed and dozy expression. She is now the best rat-catcher for miles, fiercely protective of her much larger but timid brother called Fluff, and often used to perch on top of a dog called Rex!

Gopa and Jespah

Two half-Siamese male cats from Neath named after cubs of Elsa the Lioness, whose story is told by Joy Adamson in *Living Free The Story of Elsa and Her Cubs* (1961). Elsa had three cubs, one female called Little Elsa, and two males. *Gopa* is a Swahili word meaning timid, whereas Jespah was derived from *Japhtah*, meaning 'God sets free'.

Gremlin

One of several nicknames for a black and white cat from Batley in Yorkshire. This one is used when he is being particularly naughty.

The Grinch

A strange name invented to describe the expression of a cat which appeared on the doorstep one day looking terminally fed up!

Griza

One of a family of cats from London. *Griza* is the Esperanto word for grey.

Guinea

A black and white cat who used to live in Chigwell. She was named after the vet's fee for spaying her which, in 1947, was one guinea!

Guinness

Guinness is a black polydactyl cat from London with a total of twenty-four claws and a white bib. He was named partly because of his colour, but mainly as a drinking companion for Brahms and Liszt, and Scotch and Soda.

Gussie

Gussie was rescued from Liverpool with her four kittens after being abandoned because they were not Siamese like the father. Her name was inspired by the tennis player Gertrude Augusta Moran (b.1923), known as Gorgeous Gussy after wearing lace panties designed by Teddy Tinling at Wimbledon in 1949. The cat has lived up to the name, winning several cups at cat shows near Walton-on-Thames.

Gypsy

Gypsy was a pregnant dark tortoiseshell cat rescued by the Edinburgh Cat Protection League. The name arose firstly because she was nomadic like a gypsy; secondly because of the owner's interest in English traditional dances which include a figure called gypsy; and thirdly after *Gipsy Moth IV*, the boat in which Sir Francis Chichester made the first solo voyage round the world in 1966-7.

GYPSY

Hovis

Haggis

A tabby cat from Swindon whose name was chosen to complement that of her companion who had already been christened Faggot.

Half-Pint

Not a common name, but it belongs to one cat from Aberdeen who was the runt of a litter, and to another cat from Crewe who, as a tiny kitten, was small enough to fit into a half-pint mug. The effect on the beer has not been recorded!

Harley and Davidson

A pair of cats named after the most famous and enduring American motor-cycle manufacturer. Harley-Davidson machines first appeared in 1903 and in more recent years have become known for being extraordinarily bulky. Harley is also the name of white tomcat living in Northampton.

Heineken

Not a unique name but it seemed particularly appropriate for one cat who was a great explorer and famous for 'reaching the parts other cats could not reach'. It also belongs to a cat from Bedfordshire living in a house full of companions bearing names inspired by the owner's Dutch in-laws.

Henry

This tomcat was taken in as a companion to a female already called Etta. The name seemed totally logical.

Herbaceous Border

A male cat from Tisbury in Wiltshire whose full name is actually Eric Argus Chesney Herbaceous Border!

Hermione

The replacement name chosen for Hieronymus Bosch (see below) when he was discovered to be a she.

Hieronymus Bosch

This completely wild feral cat was eventually renamed Hermione when her sex was discovered. Hieronymus Bosch (c.1460-1516) was a Dutch painter, remembered particularly for bizarre, nightmarish and gruesome pictures of monsters and devils. He has been considered the precursor of the modern surrealist movement.

Holly

A common name for kittens bought as presents for children at Christmas time, a gift which is now rightly discouraged by most animal protection organisations.

Honey

Quite a popular name, belonging to one Siamese from Ashford in Middlesex 'because she is so sweet', and also to a Persian from Brighouse who has a honey-coloured patch over one eye. It is most commonly chosen simply to describe fur colouring.

Hoover

Hoover comes from Crewe, and as with many strays, he arrived looking very thin and obviously ravenously hungry. He was named after the way in which he vacuumed up his food, and even now he seems determined to consume everything in his path.

HOOVER

Hovis

An Abbyssinin from Grimsby whose pedigree name was unpronounce-able. His owners chose a new name to reflect the colour of his fur which reminded them of a loaf of brown bread.

Hughie

Several Hughies are known! One is a dark tabby from Leicester, initially called Wee Hughie, rescued during a farm holiday on the Isle of Islay. He was amongst a litter of kittens 'going to join the Navy' (to be drowned). Another is named after a Disney cartoon character, strictly spelt Huey, who first appeared in 1938 along with Dewey and Louie as the three uncontrollable nephews of Donald Duck.

izzy

I

INDIA

Index

A name picked in desperation by an overworked librarian, inundated with cataloguing problems.

India

India is a female long-haired tabby from Nottinghamshire. She is multi-coloured, well camouflaged in the garden, and her name was chosen to remind her owner of the warmth and colours she experienced while staying in India.

Isambard Kingdom Cat I

This Bristolian cat was named in 1985 during the 150th anniversary of 'God's Wonderful Railway'. Isambard Kingdom Brunel (1806-59) was a prolific engineer, remembered particularly for his period as chief engineer of the Great Western Railway and for his three great steamships, the *Great Western* (1838), *Great Britain* (1845), and *Great Eastern* (1858).

Ishtar

An appropriate name for a cat who always seemed to be pregnant. Ishtar was the Babylonian goddess of fertility, revered as the evening manifestation of the star Venus. Her cult became widespread, extending to the whole of the Middle East, and even to Greece.

Izzy

Another pet name, this time a more manageable abbreviation for Isambard Kingdom Cat I.

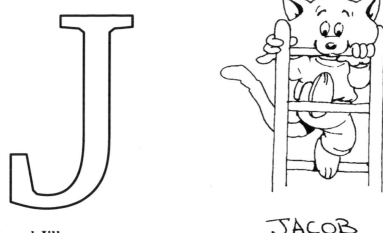

JACOB

Jack and Jill

A brother and sister from Bristol named after the nursery rhyme couple. The rhyme originated in the eighteenth century but may be even older. It was later considerably extended and published as a children's book titled *Jack and Jill, and Old Dame Gill*. The names are often used to mean just lad and lass.

Jackson

This small, black, and very pretty cat from Spain is described by his owner as a sort of feline Michael Jackson. Michael Joe Jackson (b.1958) had several hit records with his brothers as the Jacksons before becoming one of the biggest superstars of the 1980s. His album *Thriller* (1982) has sold more than 40 million copies.

Jacob

A Scottish cat with a biblical name. Jacob was the son of Isaac and Rebekah, popularly associated with the phrase Jacob's Ladder, referring to his dream of a ladder stretching up to heaven. The name is often applied to steep ladders and steps, especially nautical rope ladders.

Jaffa

Yet another orange cat, like Chivers and Pippin, named after his colouring, Jaffa being the most famous trade name for oranges.

Jake and Elwood

Jake and Elwood were characters originally created in 1978 by John Belushi and Dan Ackroyd for the American TV show *Saturday Night Live*. They were developed in 1980 for the film *The Blues Brothers,* an expensive chase comedy which was initially unsuccesful but later became a popular cult movie.

Jason

Greek mythology is a rich source for cat names. Jason was the leader of the Argonauts, a group which included Hercules, Theseus and Orpheus. They sailed in the ship *Argo* to capture the Golden Fleece, and eventually escaped with it after receiving help from Medea, the king's daughter.

Jasper

A cream Burmese, one of three brothers from Hockley in Essex, named after one of the three wise men. They were actually called Melchior, Gaspar (or Caspar), and Balthazar. Gaspar was the bringer of frankincense, and his name means 'The White One'.

Jaws

Jaws is a tomcat from Merseyside who was originally named Arthur. He earned this nickname for his prodigious appetite, obviously inherited from his grandfather, Sir Noshalot.

Jeepers

As with many kittens, Jeepers seemed to have exceptionally large eyes and his name was inspired by the song 'Jeepers, Creepers, Where d'ya Get Those Peepers?' It was written by Harry Warren and Johnny Mercer for the American film *Going Places* and was nominated for an academy award in 1938.

Jemimah

Another of the names derived from the popular Beatrix Potter children's stories. *The Tale of Jemimah Puddle-Duck* was first published in 1908.

Jeremy

Yet another name from a Beatrix Potter story. *The Tale of Mr. Jeremy Fisher* was first published in 1906.

Jervaulx

A female chocolate-licked tabby, named by a clergyman's wife after Jervaulx Abbey, the remains of a twelfth century Cistercian monastic house above the River Ure in North Yorkshire.

Jessie

Jessie is a red-haired cat from Northampton, one of twins living in an upstairs flat. Unfortunately she can no longer manage the acrobatics necessary to climb to the cat flap, so she has taken up residence with the downstairs neighbour. The name is by no means unique and also belongs to a rescued OAP cat from Larkhall in Lanarkshire.

JIMBO

Jimbo

This red cat from Northampton was such an elegant leaper that he was named after the American tennis player Jimmy Connors. James Scott Connors (b.1952) won several major titles including the men's singles at Wimbledon in 1974 and 1982.

Jo

A tabby from Plymouth, the name abbreviated from the mineral Jordanite, inspired by the owners' interest in geology. Jordanite is lead arsenic sulphide, found in the form of tabular crystals in Switzerland and Japan.

Johan Cruyff

Another cat from Bedfordshire whose name was inspired by Dutch in-laws. Johan Cruyff (b.1947) is one of the great names of football. He was European footballer of the year in 1971, 1973 and 1974, and star of the Dutch team eventually beaten by Germany in the 1974 World Cup final. He became a successful manager for Ajax of Amsterdam, and later of Barcelona.

Joshua

This is the tenuous but cleverly conceived name for a kitten whose origins were a mystery. In the bible Israel's great military leader Joshua is always described as the son of Nun, and lateral thinking converts Nun to none to nothing, referring to the nothing known about the cat's ancestry.

Josiah

A biblical name belonging to a cat from Castle Douglas in Scotland. Josiah was the son of Amon and Jedidah, and became the sixteenth King of Judah.

Julio

At least one cat is known to be named after Julio Iglesias (b.1943), the popular singer of love songs, sometimes called 'the Spanish Sinatra', who has sold more than 100 million albums. The name is also one of the Esperanto-related fore-names belonging to a Siamese cat usually known as Monte, this one in honour of Julio Baghy, a Hungarian poet and novelist.

JEEPERS

KIRI

Kali

A warlike name for a fiercely independent female cat. Kali was the Vedic or Hindu goddess of time, an early four-handed war goddess and the wife of Siva. She was also the titular goddess of the Thugs, an Indian brotherhood of robbers who practiced *thuggee*, strangling human victims in the name of religion. The sect survived until about 1880.

Kamikaze Adventurer

This chocolate tabby point Siamese lives near Croydon and was named in honour of his mischievous exploits as a kitten.

Kandi-Floss

A cream Burmese from Hockley with very silky fur. She was originally named simply Floss, after the technical name for the outer part of the silkworm's cocoon, but unlike most cat names it grew longer rather than shorter.

Keith Prowse

This comfort loving cat always takes "the best seat in the house'. He was named after Keith Prowse, the London booking agency which specialised, amongst other things, in theatre tickets.

King Arthur

This ginger tabby from Laindon in Essex was originally a thin and starving stray called Arthur. When his rescuers had finished feeding him up he became so beautiful and regal that he was promoted to King.

Kipper

Sleepy cats are not uncommon but this inactive puss spent so much time stretched out that there was serious discussion as to whether he suffered from feline sleeping sickness. He didn't!

Kiri

A beautiful blue and cream smoke Persian from Bury St Edmunds. She never stopped singing as a kitten so was named after the famous New Zealand operatic soprano Kiri Te Kanawa (b.1944). She became more widely known after singing at the wedding of the Prince and Princess of Wales.

Kisa

A black cat from Somerset with an original name reflecting his colouring, derived from the Swahili word for darkness.

Kismet

A Birman from Torquay who was the runt of a litter and required a lot of tender care. Her new owners felt they were fated to look after her and chose the name Kismet for its meaning of fate or destiny.

Kolomano

One of several Esperanto-related forenames belonging to a Siamese cat usually known as Monte, this one in honour of the Hungarian Kolomano Kalocsay, considered one of the greatest Esperanto poets.

KIPPER

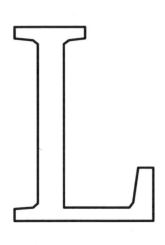

LADY

Lady

Lady was a stray but now lives near Lincoln and loves peanuts. Her name was chosen to reflect her small stature and delicate and refined nature!

Lamb Chop

A male white Persian from Rochdale. As a kitten he used to frolic like a lamb, and since he had to be weaned very early following the sad death of his mother, his face was usually covered with food.

Laurilee

This Leicestershire born foreign lilac was named after the English poet and author, a distant work colleague of the breeder. Laurie Lee (b.1914) is perhaps best remembered for *Cider with Rosie* (1959), the first of his three autobiographical books.

Lettuce

One of the names of a cat from Wiltshire which delights in the full name Lettuce Elizabethan Lily Pod Trout!

Liebniz

An attractive invented name derived from liebling, or loved one. Baron Gottfried Wilhelm von Leibniz was a noted German philosopher in the late 17th century, famous for his opposition to Descartes.

Lily Pod

Another of the names of the cat from Wiltshire christened Lettuce Elizabethan Lily Pod Trout!

Lineker

There are several cats named by football supporters after their favourite players. Gary Lineker (b.1960) played for Leicester, Everton and Barcelona before joining Tottenham Hotspur. He is currently one of England's leading goal scorers.

Little One

A stray which flew into her new owner's kitchen in Bristol and then just refused to leave. She was originally named because she seemed so tiny, but is now a real roly-poly.

Lóki

This grey and white British short-hair was rescued from a farm on the Orkneys because the farmer was afraid the kitten would eat rat poison. He inherited a wild streak from his feral mother, and was named after a Norse god to reflect the Viking connection with the Orkneys. Lóki is a culture hero in Nordic myth.

Lucky

Simply lucky to be alive after the dreadful condition in which the cat was found.

Lucy

A tabby from Plymouth, named along with Martha after engine houses at Cornish mines. The owner's husband was particularly interested in minerals and mining.

MERLIN

Magnolia Petal

There are several cats called Petal, amongst them this chocolate point Siamese from Kirkby Lonsdale. As a kitten acquired following the sad death of a cat called Blossom, she seemed so small that the owners felt she would never grow to be a complete flower.

Maisie

A tabby and white cat from Somerset, companion to Boot. Both are named after characters in Maurice Dodd's strip cartoon *The Perishers*.

Malushla

Another foreign name belonging to a Birman from Torquay. It was a name that the owner's daughter was called by an elderly lady in a residential house where she worked. Malushla is not a true Russian word, but a term of endearment rather like the English 'poppet', the nearest translation being 'my dear little thing'. The cat has since been nicknamed Cushy.

Mama's Angel

Stray cats end up with all sorts of names. This one from Sowerby in Yorkshire had been abandoned in a shed and was not much to look at, but became much loved by his adopted owner.

Mananans Mist

A foreign blue raised near Leicester whose name was inspired by the mythical god who lived on the Isle of Man and the colour of the mist often seen in the island. The Celtic sea god Mananan was the son of Lir and patron of seamen and merchants. He was also charged with weather forecasting!

Manky

This battle-scarred stray tabby from Plymouth was given a name to reflect the condition in which he was found.

Marley

A big, black cat named after the Jamaican reggae artist. Bob Marley (1945-81) was a singer, songwriter and guitarist who became a superstar in 1976. He worked with a group called the Wailers but tragically died of cancer while on tour in Germany.

Marley Wailer

Another name inspired by Bob Marley, this one belonging to an Abbyssinian who lives at San Carlos on the island of Ibiza. The Wailer part was derived from his habit of wailing, particularly for food, and has given rise to his nickname of the Prince of Wails (sic), with whom he shares a birthday.

Marmite

An excellent example of an original name chosen by a young girl to reflect a kitten's colouring. Marmite is a black cat from Birmingham, named after the well-known yeast extract.

Martha

Another tabby from Plymouth, named along with Lucy after engine houses at Cornish mines.

Mauser

A surprisingly common name belonging to at least three cats. One was owned by a military enthusiast and named after the famous German automatic pistol, a descendant of the Prussian army rifle of 1871. Another, a grey tabby from Aberdeen was originally called Skippy but renamed in recognition of her large whiskers. A third was named in the eventually forlorn hope that the kitten would become good at catching mice. It didn't!

McGinty

Cats are named after all sorts of animals, this one after a goat. The inspiration was the song 'Paddy McGinty's Goat', made popular by Val Doonican.

Meeka

This Crawley-based blue and white cat was named to reflect her meek and mild character. She always moved slowly and also earned the nickname Plod-Plod.

MINNEHAHA

Merlin

Arguably the most famous wizard of all time, and an excellent name for a cat. Merlin became a prominent figure in the legend of King Arthur and his Knights of the Round Table. It was he who proposed the trial of Excalibur, the sword in the stone, to select the king.

Mi

Another very original name with the obvious benefit that it is difficult to abbreviate! It is actually short for miles, representing the large number driven while the owners were searching for their ideal kitten.

Midas

An appropriate name for a gold tortoiseshell cat. Midas was a king in Greek mythology who was granted his wish that everything he touched might turn to gold. Unfortunately this also affected his food and drink and he soon prayed for an end to the fatal gift. He was told to bathe in the River Pactolus, which ever since has been found to be rich in gold.

Midge

Many litters include one weak and tiny kitten, and those that survive often become the most treasured cats. Midge was the runt of her litter and her name was chosen because she was so small. She now lives happily in Aberdeen.

Midnight

One of several popular names for black cats, Midnight lives near Grimsby and is absolutely jet black.

Mimi, the Dowager Duchess

A beautiful green-eyed cat from Laindon in Essex. She has a deep coat and luxurious tail, and obviously deserved a name to match.

Mimuschka

This Maine Coon kitten from Falkirk was named as a contribution to the current mood of detente, the name Russian-sounding, the cat American. She has turned out to be good natured but dumb, and is now generally referred to as Mush.

Minbu

Oddly enough Minbu is not a unique name. At least two owners of Burmese kittens have picked it independently from a map of Burma, where it is a relatively common placename. The largest is a town on the Irrawaddy River, about 250 miles north of Rangoon, quite literally on the road to Mandalay.

Minnehaha

One of four cats from Bristol named after characters from Henry Wadsworth Longfellow's poem *The Song of Hiawatha* (1855). Hiawatha was a legendary Mohawk Indian chief and Minnehaha was his Dakota wife, the arrow maker's daughter. The name means laughing water.

Mischa

A male lilac point Siamese from Chippenham, named after the son of French singer, songwriter and actor Charles Aznavour (b.1924), a friend of the owner's family.

Misty Blue

At least two female cats bear this name, a blue Burmese from Manchester and a Russian blue from Hampshire. Both were named after their colour, but the inspiration for the first was the pedigree name of My Little Blue Calypso, while the second came while the cat was playing in a shaft of sunlight which made her coat appear misty.

Mitzi

An elegant and vocal female cat named after the American actress Mitzi Gaynor (b.1930). Her real name was Francesca Mitzi Marlene de Charney von Gerber, and she is particularly remembered for her role in the film version of the musical *South Pacific* (1958).

MOSES

Mogadishu

Just like another cat called Snuff, this black kitten seemed to sneeze every time it washed its nose. The name is a wonderful example of onomatopoeia, one of the best to use a play on the word mog or moggy. Mogadishu is the capital of Somalia and lies just north of the equator on the Indian Ocean coast of North East Africa. It is now called Muqdisho.

Mole

An abbreviation of Ignatius Mole, a name chosen for a very small kitten who, when born, was blind and pink with big paws just like a mole. He still looks faintly surprised when he encounters daylight and has a rather flattened facial expression.

Monte

This Siamese lives in Oxford and his full name is Ernfrid Don-Juan Tibor Reto Julio Kolomano Ferenc de Montevideo. These are all names of distinguished people involved with the artificial universal language Esperanto. The 'surname' Montevideo was chosen to commemorate a resolution favouring Esperanto passed by UNESCO in 1954.

Moonbeam

Simply an attractive name for a black cat with big yellow eyes.

Mopsy

This stray from Lutterworth is now a companion to Topsy. Mopsy is one of the four little rabbits featured in the first of Beatrix Potter's famous children's books *The Tale of Peter Rabbit* (1901).

Mordechai

A long-haired black cat from Sidcup, companion to Golde and also named after a character in the musical *Fiddler on the Roof.*

Morio

This male chocolate point Siamese lives in Gloucestershire and was named after an uncommon plant which the owner had just seen for the first time. *Orchis morio,* the exotic green winged orchid, is native in Britain, Europe and W. Asia.

Morríghan

Rescued from a Tayside cat shelter, Morríghan was soon recognised as a proper little horror. As a black cat the witching connection was inevitable and she was named after the Celtic 'mor righan' or Great Queen known as the Phantom Queen and the goddess of war and death!

Moses

Another of the names inspired by an association of ideas. In this case the cat was delivered to his new owners in a basket, and Moses seemed an obvious choice.

Mottel

A long-haired white cat from Sidcup, companion to Golde and also named after a character in the musical *Fiddler on the Roof.*

Mouse

Several cats are perversely called Mouse, including one from Tisbury in Wiltshire. Perhaps the best justification concerns a kitten who proved extremely difficult to catch and seemed to be playing cat and mouse with his prospective new owners.

Moyshe

A male long-haired white cat from Sidcup, companion to Golde and also named after a character in the musical *Fiddler on the Roof.*

Mr. B.

This cat from Northampton is considered by his owner to be''a real tough guy'.

Mudjekeewis

Another of the four cats from Bristol named after characters from Longfellow's *The Song of Hiawatha* (1855). Mudjekeewis was Hiawatha's father.

Muffin

Yet another pet name chosen just because it sounded nice.

Mungo

A surprisingly popular name. One cat is named after her owner Mary, usually nicknamed Mungo, and another after a negro servant in the comic opera *The Padlock* by Isaac Bickerstaffe (1768). A third is named after Mungojerie in *Old Possum's Book of Practical Cats,* the classic book of verse for children by T.S. Eliot (1939), the basis for the famous Andrew Lloyd Webber musical *Cats* (1981). A fourth is a Scottish cat named after St Mungo, or St Kentigern, a missionary in Strathclyde, Cumberland, and Wales, buried in the crypt of Glasgow Cathedral.

Murgatroyd

Murgatroyd is a male cross-breed from Edinburgh, named after a toy rabbit.

Mushroom Friday

A most original name, inspired by the kitten's mother who loved to eat mushrooms when she was pregnant, the litter arriving on a Friday.

MOYSHE

NAPOLEON

Naira

The owner of this cat from Aberdeen was a business travel consultant and wanted a name connected with her work. Naira is the currency of Nigeria.

Napoleon

An extremely demanding cat, named after Napoleon Bonaparte (1769-1821). Born in Corsica, he was a notable military commander. He became Consul following a coup d'état in 1799, declared himself Emperor in 1804, ruled until overthrown at Waterloo in 1815, and died in exile on St Helena.

Nathan

Another of those name chosen purely because it sounded right. It belongs to a Siamese cat from South Wales.

Nehru

Chosen for another Siamese cat from Neath. Pundit Motilal Nehru (1861-1931) was an Indian Nationalist leader, and his son Jawarharlal (b.1889) became leader of the National Congress Party in 1942. Both were closely associated with Gandhi.

Nermal

At least two cats are called Nermal. One is a tabby and white from Mansfield, while the other lives at Frankley in Birmingham. The name is taken from the *Garfield* comic strip.

Nero

Another historical name for a cat with dictatorial tendencies. Nero was Emperor of Rome from A.D.54 and is famous for his persecution of Christians. His rule was punctuated by profligacy, assassination and murder, and he was eventually declared a public enemy by the Senate. He committed suicide in AD 68.

Nether

Named after a village in the Quantocks just to the west of Bridgwater in Somerset, by a lover of poetry. Samuel Taylor Coleridge (1772-1834) moved to Nether Stowey in the winter of 1796 and his friendship with William and Dorothy Wordsworth developed while he was there. Coleridge Cottage, on Lime Street, is now owned by the National Trust.

Netochka Nezvanova

This black and white cat from Bristol, daughter of a local stray, was named after the title of an unfinished long novel started in 1846 by Fyodor Dostoyevsky (1821-81). The name translates roughly to Nameless Nobody, but the cat is now usually nicknamed Notty.

Nickum

A mischievous cat from Leven in Fife, whose name is derived from a Scottish word. The nearest equivalent in English would probably be the word scamp.

Nig

Another of the London cats with names derived from Esperanto. Nig is an abbreviation for *nigra,* the Esperanto word meaning black.

Nikki

A seal point Siamese who lives near Chippenham in Wiltshire, named after a left-handed Yugoslavian tennis player. Nicola Pilic (b.1939) reached No. 7 in the world rankings in 1967 and turned professional the following year.

Ninja

Some cats appear to be thoroughly evil, and this Japanese name belongs to one of them. Well known today following the craze for mutant turtles, the word is derived from a particularly murderous group of ancient Japanese warriors.

Niven

David Niven (1910-83) was a popular British actor who sadly died of motor neurone disease. His real name was James David Graham Nevins but his stage name lives on with this tomcat from Wiltshire, who arrived while his owner was reading Niven's first lighthearted autobiographical book *The Moon's a Balloon* (1972).

Noggin

This name belongs to a Scottish cat named after a measure of whisky and also to an English cat named after a children's cartoon character. *Noggin the Nog* is the Norse-like hero of a series of sagas by Oliver Postgate and Peter Firmin, published in the 1960s and 1970s.

Nokomis

The third of four cats from Bristol named after characters from Longfellow's *The Song of Hiawatha* (1855). Nokomis was Hiawatha's grandmother.

Norton

Just like Harley, Davidson and Bonneville, Norton is owned by a motorcycle enthusiast. The Norton marque was named after James Lansdowne Norton (1869-1925) and the first machine appeared in 1902. The firm was taken over by Amalgamated Motor Cycles in 1952 but the name survived in later guises as Norton Villiers and Norton Villiers Triumph.

Nosey Rosie

This blue tortie Burmese from Melksham was originally called simply Rosie, but that soon developed into Nosey Rosie as her inquisitive character became apparent.

NOSEY - ROSEY

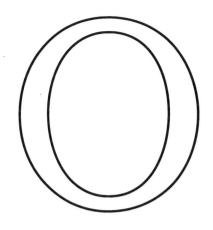

OLIVER

Octavius

Octavius was found on a pile of rubbish in a Brixton car park in October 1981, thought initially to be only a kitten but in fact already about ten years old. Although the vet gave him just two weeks to live he survived for another nine years. He had a dignified name to match his tenacity, but was known affectionately as Ocky.

Oedipuss

Another good pun on the word puss. Oedipus was a Greek legendary figure doomed to kill his father and marry his mother. He became king of Thebes, but blinded himself when he discovered the awful truth of his past.

Oliver

Amongst several cats called Oliver are a ginger and grey from Suffolk and a young kitten named by an eight year old girl from Birmingham. The name is most commonly chosen after the character created by Charles Dickens for his novel *Oliver Twist* (1838).

Oliver Digby Barrington Fairweather

This tabby point Siamese lives in Oxford. His impressive name is assembled from the middle names of four university scholars, all greatly admired by the owner.

Orlando

A relatively common name belonging to a ginger cat from Fife and also to a ginger and grey cat which lives near Bury St Edmunds. The first was named after *Orlando the Marmalade Cat,* the hero of a series of children's picture books by Kathleen Hale, published between 1938 and 1972.

PICASSO

Pablo Picasso

This post-impressionist cat from Ibiza was so named because of a white 'brush' along the ridge of his black back. He is affectionately known as Pabloid or The Lloyd. Pablo Ruiz y Picasso (1881-1973) was born at Malaga but settled in Paris. He became the most famous modern artist and was a founder of cubism.

Panda

Chosen for a black and white cat from London who has large but irregular circles around the eyes, very reminiscent of a panda.

Pandora

A Siamese rescued from Beirut, named after the lady who opened up a trunkful of woes for the world. Pandora was created by Zeus and each of the gods gave her some power to bring about the ruin of man. Her marriage dowry included a large jar or vase, now known as Pandora's box. When she opened it only hope remained inside, all the evils flew forth and have afflicted the world ever since.

Panjo

Panjo is the matron of a family of cats in London, all with names taken from the universal language Esperanto. Her name is derived from *panyo,* Esperanto for mum or mummy.

Paprika

Another of the three kittens from Gloucestershire whose mother was called Chilli Pepper. The other two are named Cayenne and Pepperoni.

Pasha

This Siamese from Ashford in Middlesex was named after the ancient Egyptian goddess Pasht. Also known as Basht or Bast, she was the daughter of Isis and a goddess of love, femininity and fertility, and had the body of a woman with the head of a cat.

Paws

Another of those names inspired by a kitten's markings, in this case belonging to a male tabby from Dumfries. He was rescued from a pet shop window when he was really too young to have been taken from his mother, and was named after his prominent white paws.

Pebbles

Yet another name chosen simply to reflect unusual and attractive colour markings. This cat had a variegated coat, rather reminiscent of the pebbles to be found on some rocky beaches.

Pegsley

This must be a unique name, belonging to a poor cat from Teddington. She has part of a back leg missing and the name just evolved from Peg, or Peg Leg.

Pelusin

Pelusin is a long-haired Persian-Chinchilla who lives in Madrid. He was named after his long and flowing coat, described by the owner as just like a river. Pélussin is in the Rhône valley, about twenty miles south of Lyon.

Penelope

A female Siamese from London named after the ubiquitous fat Aunt Penelope known to everyone in the old deep south of America. The owners describe the cat as a self-indulgent tub of lard whose purpose seems to be purely to keep food shops in business.

Pepperoni

The last of the three kittens from Gloucestershire whose mother was called Chilli Pepper.

Perchik

Perchik is another of the eight cats from Sidcup named, like Golde, after characters in the musical *Fiddler on the Roof.*

Peri

This female long-haired tabby from Scotland was given the name of a Persian fairy. The Peri appear to have been early river and forest goddesses who later became Zoroastrian female demons, and eventually good and kindly sprites.

Petra

A female Birman from Glasgow, named after a place where the owner's husband had been stationed. Petra is an ancient city in Jordan, carved from solid multicoloured rock strata. Originally a stronghold and treasure city, it became a wealthy commercial centre, had an important caravan trade, and was an early seat of Christianity. Known as the Rose City, its ruins were discovered in 1812.

Picket

Picket resides in the fire station at Weston-super-Mare. She is a tabby, now thirteen years old, who made the fire station her home during the strike of 1977. She earned her name by doing picket duties with the firemen and is now the station's official picket.

Pickwick

Pickwick lives at Corsock in Scotland and was named while the owner was listening to a serial on the radio. The Pickwick Papers is one of Charles Dickens' best known novels, first published in 1837.

PICKET

Piggy

Probably a common name since cats are famous for their voracious appetites. One kitten was named after Miss Piggy, the superstar friend of Kermit the Frog in Jim Henson's award-winning and much acclaimed television show *The Muppets* (1976-80).

Piles

As a species cats are normally known for their cleanliness, but this grubby moggy's name derives from the unwelcome piles frequently discovered by her long-suffering owners.

Pip and Squeak

A pair of dark tabby strays from Bury St Edmunds, named after comic strip characters. Pip, Squeak and Wilfred were a dog, a penguin, and a baby rabbit, featured in the *Daily Mirror* between 1919 and 1953.

Pippa

Another name which is not unique, belonging to at least two cats, one from Northampton and the other from Chigwell. The latter was named after the Piper north sea oil platform, on which the owner's son was working, fortunately some time before the Piper Alpha disaster of February 1988.

Pippin

Yet another marmalade cat with a name based on its colouring. Pippin's fur is predominantly orange, and his name was inspired by England's best flavoured dessert apple, Cox's Orange Pippin.

Plonker

Not the most complimentary name, but thoroughly earned by one cat who was a real plonker!

Plug and Socket

A pair of cats from Glasgow who were adopted from a cat league rescue centre and were believed to be brother and sister.

Polly

This tabby from Somerset has an extra thumb on each front paw. She was originally owned by a scientist who named her Polly after the prefix poly, meaning many, a subtle and ingenious reference to polydactyl. While the cat was being tended for injuries received in an argument with a rottweiler, the vet commented that the dog must have been a mess!

PEGSLEY

Pookins

Robertstown in mid-Glamorgan is the home of this cat named after a mining tool called a pookins cutter. The name was inspired by the owner's father, who used to be a miner. It is not uncommon for the cat to be discovered mining through the wrapping into an unguarded loaf of bread!

Popocatepetl

A pet name for a very active female tabby from Glasgow. Popocatepetl is an Aztec name meaning 'smoking mountain' and is a dormant volcano, forty-five miles south east of Mexico City. At 17,887 feet it is the second highest peak in Mexico, and although it last erupted in 1702, it still occasionally emits vast clouds of smoke.

Poppy

Flower names are always popular, and Poppy belongs to a black cat from Fowey and a tabby from Northampton. They were both named because they had prominent eyes, one yellow and the other green, with large black centres, just like the flower.

Porporina

This lilac point Siamese from West Glamorgan was named by an owner with fond memories of living in Italy some years ago. It is derived from the Italian word *porpora*, which means purple, and was inspired by the cat's colouring.

Portia

A female Persian from Icklingham in Suffolk. There are two famous women called Portia, both appearing in plays by Shakespeare. One was the wife of Brutus, the assassin of Julius Caesar. The second is the heroine in *The Merchant of Venice* (1596).

Posie

This moggy had ideas somewhat above her station and always appeared to be posing as if for photographs.

Prince Cha-Cha

A sleek and svelte black and white tom from Laindon, offspring of the gracious Mimi, the Dowager Duchess. He was christened when his owner was learning to dance the cha-cha.

Propellor

An extremely original behavioural name, belonging to a highly athletic cat with an exceptionally long tail which he uses to good effect whilst performing his acrobatics.

Pudding

A comparatively common name belonging to well-fed roly-poly cats including a tom from Brinsley in Nottinghamshire and a female ginger cat from Plymouth.

Pumpkin

Yet another name for an orange-coloured tom. This one lives in Wiltshire and as a kitten was noticeably very round and bright orange.

Purdey

Thetford in Norfolk is the home of this tabby, named by an enthusiastic clay-pigeon shooter and lover of fine sporting guns. James Purdey (1784-1863) was a noted gunsmith who became gunmaker to the Prince of Wales in 1857. His son, also James Purdey (1828-1909), took control of the family business in 1857, and James Purdey & Sons Ltd. are now gunmakers to the Queen. A 'purrdy' good choice!

Pushka

A long-haired black and white female stray from Canvey Island. Despite the apparently Russian origin, the name was actually made up on the spur of the moment.

PROPELLER

Pushkin

This tabby from East London had an owner who was very keen on Russian names. He (the cat not the owner) went on to become the *Cat World* / Whiskas National Pet Cat Champion in 1990. Alexander Sergeyevich Pushkin (1799-1837) is considered the national poet of Russia.

Puss in Jackboots

A neutered male from Falkirk who was originally named Smog. He turned out to be extremely domineering, and gained this nickname after seeing off a very large stray tom.

Pyewacket

Pyewacket is an ancient name for a witch's cat. Its origins are lost in time but it seemed particularly appropriate for this very black cat from Tunbridge Wells. The owners remembered the name from the cat in the film *Bell, Book and Candle*, based on a play by John van Druten. The play was a comedy hit in 1950 and the 1958 film starred James Stewart and Kim Novak.

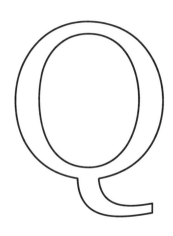

QUINCY

Quasimodo

Another poor kitten which was the runt of a litter, given an appropriate literary name. Quasimodo is the deformed bell-ringer in Victor Hugo's famous novel *Notre Dame de Paris* (1831).

Queenie Buttercup

A mock pedigree name for a moggy from Wiltshire. She was named after the character Queenie in a Liverpool electronics factory, played by Margi Clarke in the BBC television series *Making Out* (1989).

Quincy

The owners of this grey-peach tortoiseshell from Aberdeen say that she inspects and dissects everything, just like her TV namesake. *Quincy* is an American television series which first appeared in 1976. The title character is a medical examiner from the coroner's office, played by Jack Klugman. Another Scottish cat called Quincey lives at Corsock.

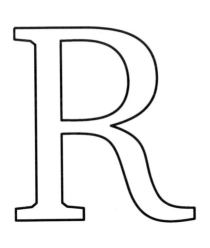

RIFF - RAFF

Rama

A stray Siamese who was given a name which means king in Thai. *Rama* also means 'the dark-coloured one' and is the name of three of the earthly incarnations of the Indian god Vishnu.

Randy Andy

The nickname of Andy Capp, a grey and white cat from Horsham, earned because of his amorous exploits.

Ranee

This queenly long-haired white cat from Newent in Gloucestershire bears the Hindu name for a queen or princess. It is sometimes written as *rani* and also refers to the wife of a rajah.

Rastus

A completely black stray with huge green eyes, found one stormy night in a tree! Owned by friends of the publisher, this beautiful and friendly cat was shot by an over-zealous gamekeeper.

Ratty

A silver sorrel Somali from Grimsby, named when she was a kitten because the owners thought she looked and moved like a rat. She later became known as Tara, socially a little more acceptable, but still 'a rat' backwards.

Rebecca

A grey and white cat from Plymouth whose name is derived from the mineral riebeckite, inspired by the owners' interest in geology. Riebeckite, or ossanite, is hydrous sodium iron silicate, found in the form of prismatic crystals in Wales and Colorado.

Red Rum II

A ginger tom from Bracknell in Berkshire, named after the famous racehorse who captured the country's imagination in the 1970s. Red Rum was a great steeplechaser who won the Grand National three times, ridden by B. Fletcher in 1973 and 1974, and by T. Stack in 1977. He also came second in 1975 and 1976.

Redvers

This tabby and white cat from Lincoln was originally named Dusty. He is rather nervous and tends to disappear whenever anyone calls, a habit which earned him this new name after Redvers Kyle, a weatherman on ITV, because 'you never see him either'.

Reto

One of several Esperanto-related forenames belonging to a Siamese cat usually known as Monte, this one in honour of Reto Rossetti, a Swiss poet, writer, translator and lecturer.

Rhubarb

Not the most complimentary of names. It was imagined to be the gist of the conversation between the newly-arrived cat and a resident dog when they first met rhubarb rhubarb rhubarb !

Rievaulx

A female Havana, named by a clergyman's wife after Rievaulx Abbey, the ruins of a twelfth or thirteenth century Cistercian abbey, just west of Helmsley in North Yorkshire.

Riff-Raff

Some animals always seem to be scruffy, no matter how well-bred!

Rifka

Another of the eight cats from Sidcup all named, like Golde, after characters in the musical *Fiddler on the Roof*.

Ripper

As a kitten Ripper demonstrated something of a destructive streak, and earned his name by shredding a new pair of curtains.

Robinson

A brave and charismatic cat from Northampton, rescued after a road traffic accident. Daniel Defoe's book *Robinson Crusoe* was first published in 1719 and has since become a classic children's story.

Rosie Pimple

One of a pair of red tabby twins from Northampton, this one named after her looks, with lots of little pimples.

Rothbury

Northumberland has a very strong folk music tradition which includes an annual festival at Rothbury. This tabby came from a nearby farm while the new owner from Somerset was on holiday at the festival. Still fairly wild, he now lives happily terrorising the local rodents near Dunster.

Ruby

A simple name inspired by the Spanish word *rubia* meaning golden or blonde. She is a ginger cat, one of three stray kittens found living on Ibiza.

Rummage

Now an inveterate explorer, Rummage is a tabby from Falkirk who earned her name as a kitten by her nervous and tentative investigation of her new home.

RUMMAGE

SID VISCIOUS

Sabiha

A Birman from Babbacombe in Devon, now usually nicknamed Sabi. She has an owner with Maltese connections and her name is derived from the Maltese for beautiful.

Sabina

Sabina is a ginger and white stray, one of three kittens which found a new home together on Ibiza. She was named after the Spanish trees on the island.

Sable

A Siamese from Ashford in Middlesex whose name was chosen because she has such beautiful fur. The sable is a small animal whose dark fur is much prized. It is also used to represent the colour black in heraldry.

Sabu

This seal point Siamese from Wiltshire was named after the boyish Indian actor Sabu Dastagir (1924-1963) who played Mowgli, the boy cub, in the 1942 American film of Rudyard Kipling's *Jungle Book*. The cat is nicknamed Madame as she is very much the ruler of the household.

Safran

Safran, like Sandal, is one of a family of cats named from the initials of words unique and specific to some event in their lives. As a kitten of only three weeks old, Safran was rescued from being put down, hence 'saved from a needle'. This approach can produce some fascinating and unique names.

Sally Pudding

One of two mischievous stray kittens living in Spain. She was originally named just Sally, derived from Scallywag, and although she was always a small cat, she eventually became rather plump from overeating and her name developed into Sally Pudding.

Salwee

A male Burmese from Chippenham. The name is derived from Salween, a district of Lower Burma on the right bank of the Salween River, which itself forms part of the border between Burma and Thailand.

Sandal

Sandal is another of the cats named from the initials of words unique and specific to their early lives. In this case she was found as a tiny kitten in Sandford Park by a girl called Alison. Like Safran, the approach has produced an attractive and unique name.

Sapphire

Another of the cat names adopted by an owner interested in minerals and geology. The sapphire is a precious stone, usually a beautiful blue.

Sarah-Jane

A very sophisticated and upper class cat from Scotland.

Sasha

A name adopted by at least two owners. One Sasha is a female pure white Russian, while another is a male lilac point Siamese. The latter lives at Chippenham in Wiltshire and was named after the popular and sexy French singer Sasha Distel (b.1933).

Sasquatch

Rather like many puppies, Sasquatch appeared to have enormous feet as a kitten. Her name is a native Indian word meaning bigfoot.

Satan

Some cats appear to be evil by nature, and Satan was a particularly appropriate name for this companion to another terror already called Ninja.

SHERPA

Scaramoosh

A popular name belonging, amongst others, to a female cat from Leven in Fife. The most obvious derivation is Scaramouch, from the Italian *scaramuccia* meaning skirmish, a character constantly cudgelled by Harlequin in commedia dell'arte. Colloquially the word means scamp or rascal.

Scats

The publisher's cat, the runt of a Dutch farm litter. Bullied unmercifully by her two larger brothers, she proved to be a delightful but utterly scatterbrained creature. Subsequently nicknamed Flopney (after her habit of 'flopping' to have her tummy tickled) and Tail-up Tilly.

Schiz and Phrenic

A pair of tortoiseshell cats from Lanarkshire named after the behaviour of one, Phrenic, an extremely freaky and suspicious feline. She was considered by their owner to be one of the scattiest and most un-together pussies ever to have lived. By contrast Schiz was a most loving and gentle cat. Sadly, they died within eight days of each other, aged fifteen.

Schoenus Niagrus

This cat from Aberdeen was unfortunate enough to arrive just as her botanist owner was working on a plant with a particularly complex name. *Schoenus niagrus* or *Schoenus nigricans* is the Black Bog-rush, a native perennial common in Scotland and Ireland.

Schroeder

A Scottish cat named after the character in the famous strip cartoon *Peanuts*. Schroeder is a friend of Lucy and Charley Brown. He idolises Beethoven and is forever playing the piano.

Scotch and Soda

Scotch and Soda are a brother and sister from London, one a male ginger tabby, the other a female long-haired tortoiseshell. Their names were chosen to continue the alcoholic association with the owner's other cats called Brahms and Liszt.

Sesamie

A clever name for a chocolate point Siamese which lives near Taunton in Somerset. It is simply an anagram of the word Siamese.

Shamu

Names encountered on favourite holidays are always popular. Shamu is a blue tabby point Birman/Siamese from Glasgow who was named after a visit to see the killer whale at Sea World in Orlando, Florida. Shamu means Precious Boy.

Shandy

Another of the apparently endless list of names which are colour derivatives. No doubt this one was dreamed up in the 'think-tank'!

Sheba

A seal point Siamese from Colinsburgh in Fife. The Queen of Sheba, strictly Sabaea and now the Yemen, visited King Solomon to see whether stories of his wisdom and riches were true. Her name is known particularly from the sinfonia 'The Arrival of the Queen of Sheba' in Handel's oratorio 'Solomon'.

Shemya Serprize

Another blue tortie Burmese named by a British Airways pilot after an airways location indicator. Shemya Island, four miles long, lies in the West Aleutian Islands of south west Alaska. Its airport was an important refuelling point on the route between the United States and the Far East.

Sherpa

Based on his remarkable ability to climb to the top of doors, this Burmese from Belfast was named after the famous mountaineer. The Sherpas are a Mongoloid mountain race from Nepal, famous for guiding expeditions in the Himalayas. The most famous is Sherpa Tensing Norkey who, with Sir Edmund Hillary, was one of the first men to reach the summit of Mount Everest in 1953.

Shoddy Body

One of several pet nicknames for an everyday black and white moggy from Peckham Rye. Her real name is Chigley.

Sid Vicious

This black, white and orange cat from Co. Antrim was an aggressive hunter of birds and rabbits and was prepared to be friendly only when she wanted to be fed. She had a really vicious streak and was named after the pop singer Sid Vicious, real name John Simon Ritchie (1957-79). He joined the Sex Pistols as guitarist in 1977 but died of a heroin overdose two years later.

Simba

This blue point Siamese from Bordon in Hampshire was named because he was big and beautiful, just like a lion.

Sir Noshalot

One of the editor's favourite names, self-explanatory for a tomcat from Merseyside with a prodigious appetite. The owner's have granted him a coat of arms consisting of a tin of catfood, supported by two tin openers rampant.

Siva

This one was a tomcat who seemed intent on the widest possible propagation of his species. Siva is the Vedic or Hindu god of reproduction and the husband of Kali. He is sometimes depicted with five heads, each with three eyes.

Skye

This chocolate point Siamese lives on Jersey and was named Skye because of her prominent sky-blue eyes. She is also known as Fanny-by-Gaslight.

Sloan

A Scottish cat who is an inveterate ranger - far and wide and often. The name is a fun derivation from the disparaging title Sloane Ranger.

Slug

Believe it or not this long-haired tabby was so deeply asleep when found in the garden that a slug had crawled over him and left a trail across his fur. He lives at Sarisbury Green in Hampshire.

Smog

Not a common name, but certainly not unique. It was chosen for one smokey grey cat whose colour reminded the owners of one of the famous London smogs. It also belongs to a tom from Falkirk, although he is more often known as Puss in Jackboots.

SOONABY

Smudge

A short-lived and purely temporary name for a cat found wandering in Suffolk with a strange pink mark around her neck. She had escaped from a zipper bag while being collected from the vet after an operation. Her owner was an eccentric old lady who cycled around with the cat in the bicycle basket, and they were reunited though an advert in the local paper.

Smudger

Smudger is another of the three stray kittens who live together on Ibiza. He was named because of a ginger smudge on his nose.

Sniffy

The runt of a litter, acquired from the RSPCA and named after a black mark on his nose and chin. Sniffy lives in Norwich and his name has proved particularly appropriate since he has a 'nose' for the good things in life such as ham, chicken, and particularly fish, on fish and chip night.

Snowdrift

Snowdrift lives near Crewe and was originally called Snowflake. Her name was changed, somewhat unflatteringly, when she became rather fat.

Snowdrop

One of several snow-related names which are fairly common choices for white cats.

Snowflake

Another of the relatively common snow-related names.

Snuff

Snuff is a tabby from Dumfries rescued by the Cat Protection League. As a kitten every time he washed his face he would sneeze loudly several times and look surprised. He grew out of the habit but the name stuck.

Snuggles

A black and white cat from Horley in Surrey, named after an endearing habit of snuggling up to her owner.

Socks

Another name based on markings, closely related to Boot and Clogs. Socks has white stockings on each leg.

Solomon

This seal point Siamese from Ashford in Middlesex was named after a garden plant. Solomon's seal, also known as David's harp, is the common name for *polygonatum x hybridum*, one of a group of herbaceous perennials of the lily family.

Soonaby

A super name for a cat which would"sooner be out than in'!

Sooty

This must be one of the most common names of all for black cats.

Sophie

A fat black cat from Berkshire. Sophie Tucker (1884-1966) was Russian-born as Sophie Kalish-Abuza, but worked in America as the heavyweight 'red hot momma' and was once described as 'a battleship with a voice like seventy trombones'. She became immensely popular in cabaret.

Spats

Another of those names, like Boot, Clogs and Socks, which reflect prominent leg markings.

Spider

A handsome short-haired black tomcat with a profile similar to the Egyptian cat on display in the British Museum. His owner's name was Webb and he soon became known as Spider Webb, or simply Spider for short.

Splodge

Not a particularly endearing name, but deliberately chosen to supplement that of his brother Smudge!

Spud

Spud is a ginger tom from Spain who was rescued from amongst several kittens on their way to the vet to be put down. He was named after his original home, a local bar called The Spud Pub.

Stig

Stig was a black cat found abandoned in an old cooker on the dump at Weston-super-Mare and taken in by the RSPCA. His new owner loved children's books and named him after the cavedweller in Clive King's immensely popular novel *Stig of the Dump* (1963).

Stoker

Stoker is short for Basingstoke and was named after his owner's least favourite city, having been lost there for two hours in what he describes as 'the most ungodly one-way traffic system ever devised'. The cat was rescued from Beirut during the Israeli siege of 1982.

Stripey

A ginger cat from Bristol named after his very prominent striped markings. He is a real beauty who has twice survived a broken leg.

Swingbin

This poor cat got its name by hanging desperately onto the sheets while attempting to climb onto the bed, all the time swinging to and fro like the lid of a flip-top rubbish bin.

Sylvester

One of the most famous cartoon cats whose name has been widely copied. Sylvester is the spluttering 'puddy tat' who made his debut in 1942 along with the lisping canary Tweety Pie, and has since appeared in a long series of Warner Brothers cartoons.

SWING-BIN

TEA · BAG

Tabitha

Tabitha is a popular name belonging to cats from Crawley in Sussex and from Plymouth. The first is a tortoiseshell named after the daughter of the friendly witch played by Elizabeth Montgomery in the TV comedy series *Bewitched,* which ran to 252 episodes between 1964 and 1971. The second is owned by a mining enthusiast who derived the name from Tabular Spar, a technical term referring to thick platy crystals.

Tabitha Twitchit

Tabitha Twitchit is named after a cat in the famous children's stories by Beatrix Potter. Mrs. Tabitha Twitchit was the mother of Mittens, Tom Kitten, and Moppet, and made her first appearance in *The Tale of Tom Kitten* (1907).

Taffeta

A cat whose owner was reminded of a taffeta skirt because of the way its fur stuck out, especially when wet.

Tail-up (Miss Elizabeth)

One cat owned by the actress Pamela Ferris who plays the part of Ma Larkin in the popular TV series *The Darling Buds of May,* based on H.E. Bates' books about the Larkin family.

Tamar

Tamar is a tabby living in the same Bristolian household as Isambard Kingdom Cat I. His name also follows the railway theme, this time derived from Brunel's famous Tamar bridge linking Devon and Cornwall, completed in 1859.

Tamara

A wandering tomcat who used to live on the Island of Mull. The owners always knew that if he didn't come home today, he'd be back 'tamara'!

Tamsin

Tamsin is the female form of Thomas and the name belongs to a blue Persian from Plymouth. She was named by a mining enthusiast after the engine house at a Cornish mine called Wheal Thomas.

Tansy

Simply a nice sounding name for a cat from Glasgow. In fact tansy is the common name of a medicinal herb, *tanacetum,* often cultivated in perennial borders.

Tarka

A female tortoiseshell cat from Madrid whose full name is actually Ambarita Tarka Del Rey. The Tarka part is after *Tarka the Otter,* the central character in the popular classic of the same name by Henry Williamson (1927).

Tasmin

This tabby from Warley was originally called Jasmine but was renamed when a new car was acquired coloured Tasman Blue. Tasmin seemed a nice mixture of the two names. The name is not unique, being shared by a beautiful long-haired grey and white 'bimbo' from Wherwell in Hampshire.

Tawny

Yet another name derived from colour association. It actually belongs to two cats, one named after the Tawny Owl and the other after Tawny Port. We must draw our own conclusions about the owners' different hobbies!

Teabag

Actually a pet name, but earned by a Burmese from Melksham which has the endearing habit of pulling used teabags out of the sink and presenting them to her owners as if she has just caught them!

Tealeaf

This female sorrel Abyssinian from Grimsby is known as Tealeaf because of her rich brown colour. Her pedigree name is actually Rosie-Lee!

TOOTS

Teddward the Terrible

A lilac point Siamese from Addington, actually named Teddy because he is the same colour as an expensive Steiff teddy bear given to his owner one Christmas. He is nicknamed Teddward the Terrible because of his destructive behaviour breaking ornaments, baby gates, and other household equipment. Margarete Steiff was a German toy manufacturer whose bears led the craze in 1903 and are now highly collectable.

Tesremos

An original name for a chocalate point Siamese from Somerset obtained by spelling the county backwards. A good idea but a technique that does not always produce good results. Try calling out for Dnalrebmuhtron or Erihskciwraw every evening!

Thomas

Worthy of inclusion here as one of the most common of all male cat names. One such tomcat is a grey tabby living in Ballymena, found abandoned in a cardboard box. The inspiration for the name is most obviously the cat in the *Tom and Jerry* cartoons.

Thumbelina

A tiny ladylike kitten that had more energy and character than any of her larger littermates. She was known as Bella for short, but tragically died after only eight weeks.

Tibor

One of several Esperanto-related forenames belonging to a Siamese cat usually known as Monte, this one in honour of Tibor Sekelj, a Yugoslavian explorer and writer.

Tigger

Another cat name taken from the popular children's stories about Winnie-the-Pooh, written by A.A. Milne. Tigger only appears in *The House at Pooh Corner,* first published in 1928.

Tiggy

A tabby stray who now lives in Plymouth. He has become so huge since being neutered that he is now usually known as Fat Cat.

Tiglath Pileser

This queenly cat from Newent in Gloucestershire was named after the vicarage cat in Agatha Christie's short story *Sanctuary.*

Timoshenko

A cat fondly remembered by a London-based owner from when she was a child. It was probably named after Simeon Konstantinovich Timoshenko (1895-1970), a marshal and Minister of Defence during World War Two. In Russia the name is not uncommon and another cat is named after the theoretician S. Timoshenko (1878-1972), noted for his *Theory of Elasticity.*

Tinker Bell

An attractive name chosen by an eight year old girl from Birmingham. Tinker Bell is a fairy in *Peter Pan,* the internationally famous children's play by J.M. Barrie. The play dates from 1904 and the story was first issued in book form in 1911.

Tiny Tim

A tragically short-lived kitten from Wingate in Co. Durham. Tiny Tim was the sadly crippled little boy in the household of Bob Cratchit, the clerk in Charles Dickens' novella *A Christmas Carol* (1843).

Titus

Titus is a dark tabby stray from Bury St Edmunds, found exploring a car park as a kitten. Titus Oates (1649-1705) was a conspirator who fabricated a Popish plot, including a Catholic rising, massacre of Protestants, burning of London, and assassination of the King (Charles II).

Tocomita

Another blue Burmese named by a British Airways pilot after an airways location indicator.

TRUBSHAW

Tokoloshe

Tokoloshe is the name of a foreign lilac from Barton St David in Somerset, a mischievous cat whose name is derived from a Bantu word meaning malevolent imp.

Tolemac

Another unusual and probably unique name derived by reversing a word. This one comes from Camelot, the name of the breeder's house in Somerset.

Tommy Pickle

One of two mischievous stray kittens living in Ibiza. This one was originally named just Tommy but he always seemed to be in some sort of trouble, and the name soon developed into Tommy Pickle.

Toots

Toots lives at Derriford near Plymouth. She is predominantly black, with some white markings, and is sister to Tiggy.

Topsy

While others bring home mice, this clever cat from Lutterworth taught itself to open the front door and then brought home another small stray which the owners adopted and subsequently called Mopsy. Topsy is the negro slave girl in Harriet Beecher Stowe's famous nursery classic *Uncle Tom's Cabin* (1851-2). In the book she is a protégée of Little Eva St Clair and claims she 'never was born I 'spect I growed'.

Tortalina

An attractive but invented name for an elegant stray tortoiseshell cat who now lives at Neath in West Glamorgan.

Tortie

A very common abbreviation of the word tortoiseshell. It is often used as a name, including a red and white cat from Northampton with a prominent 'barber pole' tail.

Trout

One of the names of a cat from Wiltshire which delights in the full name Lettuce Elizabethan Lily Pod Trout! This part is taken from the title character, an heiress, in Elizabeth Bowen's book *Eva Trout* (1969).

Trubshaw

Another cat from Castle Douglas, named after the well-known Concorde test pilot. Ernest Brian Trubshaw (b.1924) began his career in the RAF in 1942 and joined Vickers as a test pilot in 1950. He flew for them and their successors, the British Aircraft Corporation and British Aerospace, until 1980. He was awarded the OBE in 1964 and the CBE in 1970.

Truffles

An onomatopoeic name for a long-haired black cat from Chelmsford. It is thought by the owner to be unique, and is usually shortened to Truffs.

Tulip

Simply a term of endearment.

TWIGGY

Tuppence

This attractive name was chosen for one strikingly coloured cat after the old print seller's cry 'penny plain, tuppence coloured'. In Victorian times the print seller was a common street trader in London, and he was able to charge double for prints which had been coloured by hand.

Twiggy

Slim and elegant like her namesake, Twiggy is a lilac point Siamese from Leven in Fife. Twiggy was born Lesley Hornby in 1949 and became the world's most famous fashion model in the late 1960s. In 1971 she starred in *The Boyfriend,* and she is now an accomplished actress.

Tye

Another of the cats from Plymouth named by a mining enthusiast. This one is a tom whose name is taken from a mine lode.

Tzeitel

A long-haired white cat from Sidcup, companion to Golde and also named after a character in the musical *Fiddler on the Roof.* Tzeitel is a star in his own right, having appeared in one TV commercial and in several magazine advertisements.

UPPITY

Ugly

The number of uncomplimentary cat names never ceases to amaze people. It is particularly difficult to believe that any cat could deserve the name Ugly!

Umberto

An Italianate name chosen by one owner who was extremely fond of pasta. Her taste was not shared by the cat, although he eventually developed a liking for Parmesan cheese.

Uncle Sam

The popular term for the government of the United States, adopted for one very English moggy from London. The name is believed to be after a meat packer named Samuel Wilson (1766-1854), nicknamed Uncle Sam, who used to inspect meat packed for the government and mark it with the initials U.S. during the war of 1812.

Uppity

What better name could there be for this exceedingly snooty cat from Reading? He seems to spend most of his time with his nose in the air, ignoring humans and felines alike.

Uriah

A black cat named after Uriah Heep, the villainous and cunning clerk in Charles Dickens' own favourite, and partly autobiographical novel *David Copperfield* (1849-50).

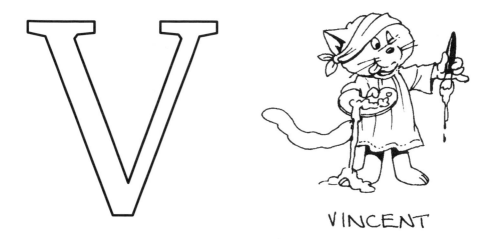

VINCENT

Velcro

Velcro was a poorly kitten just about to be taken to the vet (and oblivion) whereupon it anchored all sixteen claws into a visiting lady's sweater with such tenacity that she couldn't remove it. She became so 'attached' to the kitten that she kept it, the name being an obvious analogy to the ubiquitous fastening strip. The name is not unique, it also belongs to a cat from Mansfield whose real name is Sophie.

Vincent

A chocolate Burmese living on Jersey, also a black and white tom from Aberystwyth. The latter was a stray driven by the pain of ear mites to destroy his own left ear. The name is pitifully obvious but the cat is now cured and blissfully happy. Vincent van Gogh (1853-90) was a Dutch artist, famous for his post-impressionist paintings and for cutting off his own ear. At the time of writing, his painting of Dr. Gachet holds the world auction record of $82.5m.

Vita

This cat now lives in Cheltenham but was brought south from Scotland as a kitten, travelling in a biscuit box. The name was derived from McVitie's biscuits.

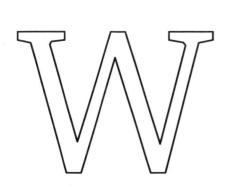

Wellie

A tabby from Crawley who was actually named Ellie but renamed Wellie to reflect her love of paddling in the bath.

Wellington

The owner was a long-term fan of Maurice Dodd's strip cartoon *The Perishers* and much preferred dogs. He decided that whatever the kids brought home it would have to be named after the cartoon character Wellington, the freckled keeper of an old English sheepdog called Boot.

Wenonah

The last of the four cats from Bristol named after characters from Longfellow's poem *The Song of Hiawatha* (1855). Wenonah was Hiawatha's mother, the first-born daughter of Nokomis.

Wild Woman of Wonga

A Burmese from Belfast whose real name is Cleopatra. She is a daft cat and earned this pet name after an equally daft 1950s B movie.

Wilhelmina

This tabby and white cat from Lincoln was going to be called Holy Queen but a neighbour's daughter mispronounced that as Holland Queen, which brought to mind Queen Wilhelmina of the Netherlands. Wilhelmina (1880-1962) was a daughter of William III and became Queen in 1890. She abdicated in favour of her own daughter, Juliana, in 1948.

Willumena

A ginger cat from Torquay originally thought to be a tom and called Pussy Cat Willum. The name was changed to Willumena when her sex was discovered.

Winchester Taxrebate

This seal tabby point Siamese is owned by an enthusiastic clay pigeon shooter from Thetford. She is named partly after the famous sporting rifle and partly after a welcome gift just received from the Inland Revenue. Oliver Fisher Winchester (1810-80), an American industrialist and arms manufacturer, developed the famous Winchester repeating rifle in about 1866.

Winnie

Named after Winnie, wife of the African National Congress leader Nelson Mandela. The cat is 'female, black and spirited'.

Winston

This name, inspired by Winston Churchill, was recalled by a correspondent from Oxford. It belonged to a wartime cat and must then have been a very common name. As with other unfortunate pets during the war, the cat eventually had to be destroyed due to the unavailability of food.

Wispy

A name chosen by an owner from Tunbridge Wells to conform with other five letter cat names. It was inspired by will-o'-the-wisp, a name for an elusive person.

Wobbly

Wobbly is an old and timid stray tom, now rescued and a much loved cat. He was rather rheumatic and of unsteady gait, hence his unusual name.

WOBBLY

Woody

A tabby who lives near Swindon found sleeping as a stray in a pile of wood in the new owner's shed.

Woody Bio Baby

The result of an illicit liaison between a pedigree Persian and an unknown moggy. This beautiful cat was named after a new garden fertiliser which was being tested at the time the kittens were born.

Wookie

Wookie is another of the cats about which little is known. The name is believed to have been chosen after one of the characters in the popular film *Star Wars*.

Wot-Not

This name was chosen for a Scottish cat who was daughter to Bog and Phrenic. With parent's names like that she was bound to be a real wot-not!

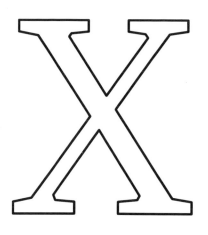

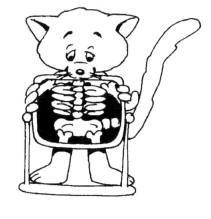

X - RAY

X-Ray

A highly imaginative name for a rather aloof cat which appears to look right through you on first acquaintance!

Xerox

This fun name was earned by a female stray who just kept right on reproducing!

Xerxes

Another cat with a rather grand historical name. Xerxes spent twelve years as Viceroy at Babylon and became King of Persia in 485 BC. He is mainly known for his invasion of Greece and ruled until assasinated by Arbatanus in 465 BC.

Xmas

This stray might equally have been called Holly. He was found on Christmas day under a frost covered caravan, and his rather red nose reminded his new owners of a holly berry.

YENTE

Yegen

A Turkish Van female from Bath was given this name to relect her relationship as niece to Tuzlu, a fellow resident. *Yegen* is a Turkish word meaning nephew or niece.

Yente

This grey and white female from Sidcup is yet another companion to Golde, again named after a character from *Fiddler on the Roof*. Yente is being groomed for stardom, and has already made her debut in one of the Take a Break (Kit-Kat) TV commercials.

Yeti

A tabby and white tom from Eastbourne whose name was chosen by a four-year old girl, and also a white long-haired cat, both named after the mysterious mythical Abominable Snowman of the Himalayas.

Yoffle

Yoffle is the wise looking bird in the Bagpuss series of children's books by Oliver Postgate.

Yuli

A familiar form of Juliet, the original name of this ginger and white female from Madrid.

ZEPPELIN

Zachary

Yet another cat named after a film star, this time the American actor Zachary Scott (1914-65).

Zebby

This name belongs to a Burmese from Icklingham in Suffolk, and is also the nickname of a tomcat called Zebedee. He was named after the bee created by Eric Thompson for the children's television series *Magic Roundabout*. First broadcast in 1965, it became a cult programme for adults in the late sixties and early seventies.

Zeke

A name associated indelibly with film "Westerns'. At least one of the gun-slinging customers in a bar room brawl scene would be called Zeke!

Zeppelin

A name belonging to both a Siamese from Leicestershire and an ordinary London moggy. The latter was a stray whose shape reminded his new owners of the Zeppelin airships. Ferdinand von Zeppelin (1838-1917) was a German soldier and inventor of the first rigid-frame airships. They became the pride of Germany between the wars but were grounded following the dramatic crash of the Hindenburg in New Jersey in 1937.

Zero

Little is known about this cat, except that the name was inspired by a song called 'Zero She Flies'.

Zia

Zia is a Burmese living near Bury St. Edmunds. The name is probably best known for President Zia of Pakistan.

Ziggy

This blue Burmese from Icklingham used to zigzag madly around as a kitten, and was given a name to match. Despite being somewhat older, the mad behaviour still persists.

Zingo

Another of the London cats with names derived from Esperanto. Zingo is an abbreviation for *zingibro,* the Esperanto word meaning ginger.

Zinziber

Zinziber is a ginger stray from Neath in South Wales whose name was half-remembered, some years after the owner worked for a pharmacist, as being Latin for ginger. The correct word would actually be *zingiber.*

Zöe

Zöe is simply an attractive female name, belonging to a Burmese who lives at Icklingham in Suffolk.

'Tailpiece'

The publishers wish to thank the many people who responded to the initial advertisement in *Cat World* and all those who, during subsequent conversations, very kindly provided a great deal of the interesting material for this book. We already knew that many cats had unusual names but we were still amazed by the diversity contained in the letters and comments we received.

Despite our efforts, it is quite clear that we have barely 'scratched the surface', and we would be delighted to hear from any reader who would like their cat's name(s) to be considered for inclusion in any further volume which may be published. Please write to:

The Bucklebury Press
1 Bucklebury Place
Upper Woolhampton
Reading
Berkshire
RG7 5UD

 # 'Paw-Note'

An <u>exclusive 'CAT-A-LIST' T-shirt</u> is available depicting the cat characters illustrated on the front and rear covers of this book. A special order form is included on the following page.

T-SHIRT FRONT

T-SHIRT BACK

JAKE AND ELWOOD

T-SHIRT ORDER FORM

Made from 100% cotton, this handsome T-Shirt carries two different and delightful cat illustrations drawn by Colin Petty. The T-Shirt is available in two sizes (large and extra large) for just £6.50 plus packing and postage.

TERMS AND CONDITIONS

i)   Please allow 28 days for delivery.

ii)   Orders can only be accepted if accompanied by a remittance for the full amount (**£6.50**), plus postage and packing at £0.75 per T-Shirt ordered.

iii) All cheques should be crossed and made payable to **THE BUCKLEBURY PRESS**; please write your name and address on the reverse of cheques and postal orders.

iv)   The offer is open to U.K. residents only.

Please print your name and address in CAPITAL letters:

QUANTITY:-

LARGE: [ ]   EXTRA LARGE: [ ]

Name (Mr/Mrs/Ms) _____

Address _____

_____

_____

County:_____Postcode:_____

Mallo
CAESAR
J.J.
CLEO
Timmy
Sugar!
GERALD!
Sasha
Napoleon
Paddy
Cheeky
Scar!
Murphy
Sherlock
Selby
Smokey
MR ED
Tabitha
Snooky
PINKY
MISTY!
JET
Sooty
Cleo
Sage
Novo
Napoleon